MznLnx

Missing Links Exam Preps

Exam Prep for

Managing Today

Robbins, 2nd Edition

The MznLnx Exam Prep is your link from the texbook and lecture to your exams.
The MznLnx Exam Preps are unauthorized and comprehensive reviews of your textbooks.

All material provided by MznLnx and Rico Publications (c) 2010
Textbook publishers and textbook authors do not particpate in or contribute to these reviews.

MznLnx

Rico
Publications

Exam Prep for Managing Today
2nd Edition
Robbins

Publisher: Raymond Houge
Assistant Editor: Michael Rouger
Text and Cover Designer: Lisa Buckner
Marketing Manager: Sara Swagger
Project Manager, Editorial Production: Jerry Emerson
Art Director: Vernon Lowerui

Product Manager: Dave Mason
Editorial Assitant: Rachel Guzmanji
Pedagogy: Debra Long
Cover Image: Jim Reed/Getty Images
Text and Cover Printer: City Printing, Inc.
Compositor: Media Mix, Inc.

(c) 2010 Rico Publications
ALL RIGHTS RESERVED. No part of this work
covered by the copyright may be reproduced or
used in any form or by an means--graphic, electronic,
or mechanical, including photocopying, recording,
taping, Web distribution, information storage, and
retrieval systems, or in any other manner--without the
written permission of the publisher.

Printed in the United States
ISBN:

For more information about our products, contact us at:
Dave.Mason@RicoPublications.com

For permission to use material from this text or
product, submit a request online to:
Dave.Mason@RicoPublications.com

Contents

CHAPTER 1
Welcome to the Changing World of Work — 1

CHAPTER 2
Managing Organizations and People: Who, What, and Why? — 11

CHAPTER 3
Making Decisions — 18

CHAPTER 4
Monitoring the Environment — 26

CHAPTER 5
Planning Systems — 34

CHAPTER 6
Monitoring Performance Through Control Systems — 41

CHAPTER 7
Technology and the Design of Work Processes — 49

CHAPTER 8
Organization Design — 60

CHAPTER 9
Managing Human Resources — 65

CHAPTER 10
Understanding Groups and Developing Effective Teams — 80

CHAPTER 11
Creating and Sustaining the Organization`s Culture — 86

CHAPTER 12
Understanding the Basics of Human Behavior — 88

CHAPTER 13
Work Motivation and Rewards — 97

CHAPTER 14
Basic Issues in Leadership — 105

CHAPTER 15
Contemporary Issues in Leadership — 109

CHAPTER 16
Building Trust — 112

CHAPTER 17
Developing Interpersonal Skills — 114

CHAPTER 18
Managing Change: Revisiting the Changing World of Work — 121

ANSWER KEY — 128

TO THE STUDENT

COMPREHENSIVE

The *MznLnx* Exam Prep series is designed to help you pass your exams. Editors at MznLnx review your textbooks and then prepare these practice exams to help you master the textbook material. Unlike study guides, workbooks, and practice tests provided by the texbook publisher and textbook authors, *MznLnx* gives you **all** of the material in each chapter in exam form, not just samples, so you can be sure to nail your exam.

MECHANICAL

The MznLnx Exam Prep series creates exams that will help you learn the subject matter as well as test you on your understanding. Each question is designed to help you master the concept. Just working through the exams, you gain an understanding of the subject--its a simple mechanical process that produces success.

INTEGRATED STUDY GUIDE AND REVIEW

MznLnx is not just a set of exams designed to test you, its also a comprehensive review of the subject content. Each exam question is also a review of the concept, making sure that you will get the answer correct without having to go to other sources of material. You learn as you go! Its the easiest way to pass an exam.

HUMOR

Studying can be tedious and dry. MznLnx's instructional design includes moderate humor within the exam questions on occassion, to break the tedium and revitalize the brain

Chapter 1. Welcome to the Changing World of Work

1. _____ is the process of social and economic change whereby a human group is transformed from a pre-industrial society into an industrial one. It is a part of a wider modernization process, where social change and economic development are closely related with technological innovation, particularly with the development of large-scale energy and metallurgy production. It is the extensive organization of an economy for the purpose of manufacturing.
   a. A Stake in the Outcome
   b. AAAI
   c. A4e
   d. Industrialization

2. The 'business case for _____', theorizes that in a global marketplace, a company that employs a diverse workforce (both men and women, people of many generations, people from ethnically and racially diverse backgrounds etc.) is better able to understand the demographics of the marketplace it serves and is thus better equipped to thrive in that marketplace than a company that has a more limited range of employee demographics.

   An additional corollary suggests that a company that supports the _____ of its workforce can also improve employee satisfaction, productivity and retention.

   a. Virtual team
   b. Trademark
   c. Kanban
   d. Diversity

3. A _____ in today's workforce is an individual that is valued for their ability to interpret information within a specific subject area. They will often advance the overall understanding of that subject through focused analysis, design and/or development. They use research skills to define problems and to identify alternatives.
   a. Customer satisfaction
   b. Business rule
   c. Knowledge worker
   d. Career development

4. The _____ is the labour pool in employment. It is generally used to describe those working for a single company or industry, but can also apply to a geographic region like a city, country, state, etc. The term generally excludes the employers or management, and implies those involved in manual labour.
   a. Work-life balance
   b. Workforce
   c. Division of labour
   d. Pink-collar worker

5. _____ according to Onuoha (2007) is the practice of starting new organizations or revitalizing mature organizations, particularly new businesses generally in response to identified opportunities. _____ is often a difficult undertaking, as a vast majority of new businesses fail. Entrepreneurial activities are substantially different depending on the type of organization that is being started.
   a. Entrepreneurship
   b. A4e
   c. AAAI
   d. A Stake in the Outcome

6. _____ is the temporary suspension or permanent termination of employment of an employee or (more commonly) a group of employees for business reasons, such as the decision that certain positions are no longer necessary or a business slow-down or interruption in work. Originally the term '_____' referred exclusively to a temporary interruption in work, as when factory work cyclically falls off. However, in recent times the term can also refer to the permanent elimination of a position.
   a. Wrongful dismissal
   b. Layoff
   c. Termination of employment
   d. Retirement

7. In decision theory and estimation theory, the _____ of an estimator, $\hat{\theta}$, of an unknown parameter of the distribution, θ, is the expected value of the loss function

$$R(\theta, \hat{\theta}) = \mathbb{E}_\theta L(\theta, \hat{\theta}) = \int L(\theta, \hat{\theta}) \, dP_\theta.$$

where dP_θ is a probability measure parametrized by θ.

- For a scalar parameter θ and a quadratic loss function,

$$L(\theta, \hat{\theta}) = (\theta - \hat{\theta})^2$$

the _____ function becomes the mean squared error of the estimate,

$$R(\theta, \hat{\theta}) = E_\theta (\theta - \hat{\theta})^2$$

- In density estimation, the unknown parameter is probability density itself. The loss function is typically chosen to be a norm in an appropriate function space. For example, for L^2 norm,

$$L(f, \hat{f}) = \|f - \hat{f}\|_2^2$$

the _____ function becomes the mean integrated squared error

$$R(f, \hat{f}) = E\|f - \hat{f}\|^2$$

a. Linear model
b. Risk
c. Financial modeling
d. Risk aversion

8. An _____ is a person who has possession of an enterprise and assumes significant accountability for the inherent risks and the outcome. It is an ambitious leader who combines land, labor, and capital to create and market new goods or services. The term is a loanword from French and was first defined by the Irish economist Richard Cantillon.
a. AAAI
b. A4e
c. A Stake in the Outcome
d. Entrepreneur

9. _____ is the incidence or process of transferring ownership of a business, enterprise, agency or public service from the public sector (government) to the private sector (business.) In a broader sense, _____ refers to transfer of any government function to the private sector including governmental functions like revenue collection and law enforcement.

a. 1990 Clean Air Act
b. Performance reports
c. 28-hour day
d. Privatization

10. _____ is an advertisement in which a particular product specifically mentions a competitor by name for the express purpose of showing why the competitor is inferior to the product naming it.

This should not be confused with parody advertisements, where a fictional product is being advertised for the purpose of poking fun at the particular advertisement, nor should it be confused with the use of a coined brand name for the purpose of comparing the product without actually naming an actual competitor. ('Wikipedia tastes better and is less filling than the Encyclopedia Galactica.')

In the 1980s, during what has been referred to as the cola wars, soft-drink manufacturer Pepsi ran a series of advertisements where people, caught on hidden camera, in a blind taste test, chose Pepsi over rival Coca-Cola.

a. 1990 Clean Air Act
b. 28-hour day
c. Comparative advertising
d. 33 Strategies of War

11. The _____ captures an expanded spectrum of values and criteria for measuring organizational success: economic, ecological and social. With the ratification of the United Nations and ICLEI _____ standard for urban and community accounting in early 2007, this became the dominant approach to public sector full cost accounting. Similar UN standards apply to natural capital and human capital measurement to assist in measurements required by _____, e.g. the ecoBudget standard for reporting ecological footprint.
a. 28-hour day
b. 33 Strategies of War
c. 1990 Clean Air Act
d. Triple bottom line

12. _____ is subcontracting a process, such as product design or manufacturing, to a third-party company. The decision to outsource is often made in the interest of lowering cost or making better use of time and energy costs, redirecting or conserving energy directed at the competencies of a particular business, or to make more efficient use of land, labor, capital, (information) technology and resources. _____ became part of the business lexicon during the 1980s.

a. Opinion leadership
b. Outsourcing
c. Operant conditioning
d. Unemployment insurance

13. A _____ is a process in which a potential employee is evaluated by an employer for prospective employment in their company, organization and was established in the late 16th century.

A _____ typically precedes the hiring decision, and is used to evaluate the candidate. The interview is usually preceded by the evaluation of submitted résumés from interested candidates, then selecting a small number of candidates for interviews.

a. Split shift
b. Supported employment
c. Job interview
d. Payrolling

14. In game theory, an _____ is a set of moves or strategies taken by the players, or their payoffs resulting from the actions or strategies taken by all players. The two are complementary in that given knowledge of the set of strategies of all players, the final state of the game is known, as are any relevant payoffs. In a game where chance or a random event is involved, the _____ is not known from only the set of strategies, but is only realized when the random event(s) are realized.

a. A Stake in the Outcome
b. A4e
c. AAAI
d. Outcome

15. A _____ is a professional who provides advice in a particular area of expertise such as management, accountancy, the environment, entertainment, technology, law , human resources, marketing, medicine, finance, economics, public affairs, communication, engineering, sound system design, graphic design, or waste management.

A _____ is usually an expert or a professional in a specific field and has a wide knowledge of the subject matter. A _____ usually works for a consultancy firm or is self-employed, and engages with multiple and changing clients.

a. 28-hour day
b. 1990 Clean Air Act
c. Consultant
d. 33 Strategies of War

16. _____ is a business management strategy aimed at embedding awareness of quality in all organizational processes. _____ has been widely used in manufacturing, education, hospitals, call centers, government, and service industries, as well as NASA space and science programs.

As defined by the International Organization for Standardization (ISO):

> '_____ is a management approach for an organization, centered on quality, based on the participation of all its members and aiming at long-term success through customer satisfaction, and benefits to all members of the organization and to society.' ISO 8402:1994

One major aim is to reduce variation from every process so that greater consistency of effort is obtained. (Royse, D., Thyer, B., Padgett D., ' Logan T., 2006)

a. Total quality management
b. 28-hour day
c. 1990 Clean Air Act
d. Quality management

17. _____ is the process of comparing the cost, cycle time, productivity, or quality of a specific process or method to another that is widely considered to be an industry standard or best practice. Essentially, _____ provides a snapshot of the performance of your business and helps you understand where you are in relation to a particular standard. The result is often a business case for making changes in order to make improvements.
    a. Complementors
    b. Cost leadership
    c. Competitive heterogeneity
    d. Benchmarking

18. _____ is a process or productivity improvement tool intended to have a stable and consistent growth and improvement of all the segments of a process or processes. _____ ensures the process stabilization and further improvement. When an organization's growth and development is intended, identification of all the processes and development of a measurement analysis of each process step is necessary.

a. 1990 Clean Air Act
b. 33 Strategies of War
c. 28-hour day
d. Continual improvement

19. _____ can be considered to have three main components: quality control, quality assurance and quality improvement. _____ is focused not only on product quality, but also the means to achieve it. _____ therefore uses quality assurance and control of processes as well as products to achieve more consistent quality.
   a. 28-hour day
   b. Total quality management
   c. 1990 Clean Air Act
   d. Quality management

20. The _____ assessment is a psychometric questionnaire designed to measure psychological preferences in how people perceive the world and make decisions.[1] These preferences were extrapolated from the typological theories originated by Carl Gustav Jung, as published in his 1921 book Psychological Types . The original developers of the personality inventory were Katharine Cook Briggs and her daughter, Isabel Briggs Myers. They began creating the indicator during World War II, believing that a knowledge of personality preferences would help women who were entering the industrial workforce for the first time identify the sort of war-time jobs where they would be 'most comfortable and effective'.[xiii] The initial questionnaire grew into the _____, which was first published in 1962.
   a. 33 Strategies of War
   b. 28-hour day
   c. 1990 Clean Air Act
   d. Myers-Briggs Type Indicator

21. _____ is something that a firm can do well and that meets the following three conditions:

Competencies are things that companys execute well across several business units or product sectors.

Firms usually have few competencies, but these are usually less liable to change rapidly.

1. It provides consumer benefits
2. It is not easy for competitors to imitate
3. It can be leveraged widely to many products and markets.

A _____ can take various forms, including technical/subject matter know-how, a reliable process and/or close relationships with customers and suppliers (Mascarenhas et al. 1998.)

a. Learning-by-doing
b. Dominant Design
c. NAIRU
d. Core competency

22. _____ refers to increasing the spiritual, political, social or economic strength of individuals and communities. It often involves the empowered developing confidence in their own capacities.

The term Human _____ covers a vast landscape of meanings, interpretations, definitions and disciplines ranging from psychology and philosophy to the highly commercialized Self-Help industry and Motivational sciences.

a. AAAI
b. A4e
c. Empowerment
d. A Stake in the Outcome

23. _____ is a concept in ethics with several meanings. It is often used synonymously with such concepts as responsibility, answerability, enforcement, blameworthiness, liability and other terms associated with the expectation of account-giving. As an aspect of governance, it has been central to discussions related to problems in both the public and private (corporation) worlds.
a. Usury
b. A Stake in the Outcome
c. Accountability
d. A4e

24. _____ is the probability that an individual will keep his or her job; a job with a high level of _____ is such that a person with the job would have a small chance of becoming unemployed.

_____ is dependent on economy, prevailing business conditions, and the individual's personal skills. It has been found that people have more _____ in times of economic expansion and less in times of a recession.

a. Job security
b. Multiple careers
c. Just cause
d. Hygiene factors

Chapter 1. Welcome to the Changing World of Work

25. _____ is an organization's process of defining its strategy and making decisions on allocating its resources to pursue this strategy, including its capital and people. Various business analysis techniques can be used in _____, including SWOT analysis (Strengths, Weaknesses, Opportunities, and Threats) and PEST analysis (Political, Economic, Social, and Technological analysis) or STEER analysis involving Socio-cultural, Technological, Economic, Ecological, and Regulatory factors and EPISTEL (Environment, Political, Informatic, Social, Technological, Economic and Legal)

_____ is the formal consideration of an organization's future course. All _____ deals with at least one of three key questions:

1. 'What do we do?'
2. 'For whom do we do it?'
3. 'How do we excel?'

In business _____, the third question is better phrased 'How can we beat or avoid competition?'. (Bradford and Duncan, page 1.)

a. 33 Strategies of War
b. 28-hour day
c. 1990 Clean Air Act
d. Strategic planning

26. A _____ is a form of periodic payment from an employer to an employee, which may be specified in an employment contract. It is contrasted with piece wages, where each job, hour or other unit is paid separately, rather than on a periodic basis.

From the point of a view of running a business, _____ can also be viewed as the cost of acquiring human resources for running operations, and is then termed personnel expense or _____ expense.

a. Human resources
b. Salary
c. Human resource management
d. Training and development

27. _____ is a term defined by the Oxford English Dictionary as an individual's 'course or progress through life '. It is usually considered to pertain to remunerative work (and sometimes also formal education.)

The etymology of the term is somewhat ironic in that it comes from the Latin word carrera, which means race .

a. Nursing shortage
b. Career planning
c. Spatial mismatch
d. Career

Chapter 2. Managing Organizations and People: Who, What, and Why?   11

1. A _____ or chief operations officer is a corporate officer responsible for managing the day-to-day activities of the corporation and for operations management (OM.) The _____ is one of the highest-ranking members of an organization's senior management, monitoring the daily operations of the company and reporting to the board of directors and the top executive officer, usually the chief executive officer (CEO.) The _____ is usually an executive or senior officer.
   a. Value based pricing
   b. Supervisory board
   c. Product innovation
   d. Chief operating officer

2. _____ is the term used for the chief executive of many limited companies in the United Kingdom, Commonwealth and some other English speaking countries. The title reflects his or her role as both a member of the Board of Directors but also as the senior manager.

   In larger organisations, including investment banks and other financial institutions, '_____' does not refer to the chief executive but can rather refer to the head of a major business unit.

   a. Chief technology officer
   b. Managing director
   c. Hotel manager
   d. General Manager

3. In statistics, _____ is:

   - the arithmetic _____
   - the expected value of a random variable, which is also called the population _____.

   It is sometimes stated that the '_____' _____s average. This is incorrect if '_____' is taken in the specific sense of 'arithmetic _____' as there are different types of averages: the _____, median, and mode. Other simple statistical analyses use measures of spread, such as range, interquartile range, or standard deviation. For a real-valued random variable X, the _____ is the expectation of X. Note that not every probability distribution has a defined _____; see the Cauchy distribution for an example.

   a. Mean
   b. Correlation
   c. Control chart
   d. Statistical inference

Chapter 2. Managing Organizations and People: Who, What, and Why?

4. The _____ captures an expanded spectrum of values and criteria for measuring organizational success: economic, ecological and social. With the ratification of the United Nations and ICLEI _____ standard for urban and community accounting in early 2007, this became the dominant approach to public sector full cost accounting. Similar UN standards apply to natural capital and human capital measurement to assist in measurements required by _____, e.g. the ecoBudget standard for reporting ecological footprint.

   a. 28-hour day
   b. 1990 Clean Air Act
   c. 33 Strategies of War
   d. Triple bottom line

5. A _____ is a list of the general tasks and responsibilities of a position. Typically, it also includes to whom the position reports, specifications such as the qualifications needed by the person in the job, salary range for the position, etc. A _____ is usually developed by conducting a job analysis, which includes examining the tasks and sequences of tasks necessary to perform the job.

   a. Recruitment advertising
   b. Job description
   c. Recruitment Process Insourcing
   d. Recruitment

6. _____ is a civil designation for persons who are incorporated in a fixed or permanent way to a society or group: regular member of the working staff, permanent staff distinguished from a supernumerary.

   The term '_____' and its counterpart, 'supernumerary,' originated in Spanish and Latin American academy and government; it is now also used in countries all over the world, such as France, the U.S., England, Italy, etc.

   There are _____ members of surgical organizations, of universities, of gastronomical associations, etc.

   a. Affiliation
   b. Adam Smith
   c. Abraham Harold Maslow
   d. Numerary

7. _____ is one of the managerial functions like planning, organizing, staffing and directing. It is an important function because it helps to check the errors and to take the corrective action so that deviation from standards are minimized and stated goals of the organization are achieved in desired manner. According to modern concepts, _____ is a foreseeing action whereas earlier concept of _____ was used only when errors were detected. _____ in management means setting standards, measuring actual performance and taking corrective action.

Chapter 2. Managing Organizations and People: Who, What, and Why? 13

   a. Control
   b. Decision tree pruning
   c. Turnover
   d. Schedule of reinforcement

8. In politics, a _____, (by metaphor with the carved _____ at the prow of a sailing ship), is a person who holds an important title or office yet executes little actual power, most commonly limited by convention rather than law. Common _____s include constitutional monarchs, such as: Queen Elizabeth II, the Emperor of Japan, or presidents in parliamentary democracies, such as the President of Israel.

While the authority of a _____ is in practice generally symbolic, public opinion, respect for the office or the office holder and access to high levels of government can give them significant influence on events.

   a. 28-hour day
   b. Figurehead
   c. 33 Strategies of War
   d. 1990 Clean Air Act

9. _____ can be regarded as an outcome of mental processes (cognitive process) leading to the selection of a course of action among several alternatives. Every _____ process produces a final choice. The output can be an action or an opinion of choice.
   a. 1990 Clean Air Act
   b. Decision making
   c. 33 Strategies of War
   d. 28-hour day

10. An _____ is a person who has possession of an enterprise and assumes significant accountability for the inherent risks and the outcome. It is an ambitious leader who combines land, labor, and capital to create and market new goods or services. The term is a loanword from French and was first defined by the Irish economist Richard Cantillon.
   a. Entrepreneur
   b. AAAI
   c. A Stake in the Outcome
   d. A4e

11. A _____ is a change implemented to address a weakness identified in a management system. Normally _____s are implemented in response to a customer complaint, abnormal levels of internal nonconformity, nonconformities identified during an internal audit or adverse or unstable trends in product and process monitoring such as would be identified by SPC.

The process of determining a _____ requires identification of actions that can be taken to prevent or mitigate the weakness.

a. 28-hour day
b. Zero defects
c. 1990 Clean Air Act
d. Corrective action

12. '_____' refers to mental and communicative algorithms applied during social communications and interactions in order to reach certain effects or results. The term '_____' is used often in business contexts to refer to the measure of a person's ability to operate within business organizations through social communication and interactions. _____ are how people relate to one another.

a. Interpersonal skills
b. A Stake in the Outcome
c. AAAI
d. A4e

13. _____ refers to the movement of cash into or out of a business or financial product. It is usually measured during a specified, finite period of time. Measurement of _____ can be used

- to determine a project's rate of return or value. The time of _____s into and out of projects are used as inputs in financial models such as internal rate of return, and net present value.
- to determine problems with a business's liquidity. Being profitable does not necessarily mean being liquid. A company can fail because of a shortage of cash, even while profitable.
- as an alternate measure of a business's profits when it is believed that accrual accounting concepts do not represent economic realities. For example, a company may be notionally profitable but generating little operational cash (as may be the case for a company that barters its products rather than selling for cash.) In such a case, the company may be deriving additional operating cash by issuing shares evaluating default risk, re-investment requirements, etc.

_____ is a generic term used differently depending on the context. It may be defined by users for their own purposes.

a. Cash flow
b. Sweat equity
c. Gross profit
d. Gross profit margin

Chapter 2. Managing Organizations and People: Who, What, and Why?

14. The 'business case for _____', theorizes that in a global marketplace, a company that employs a diverse workforce (both men and women, people of many generations, people from ethnically and racially diverse backgrounds etc.) is better able to understand the demographics of the marketplace it serves and is thus better equipped to thrive in that marketplace than a company that has a more limited range of employee demographics.

An additional corollary suggests that a company that supports the _____ of its workforce can also improve employee satisfaction, productivity and retention.

   a. Trademark
   b. Kanban
   c. Diversity
   d. Virtual team

15. _____ refers to increasing the spiritual, political, social or economic strength of individuals and communities. It often involves the empowered developing confidence in their own capacities.

The term Human _____ covers a vast landscape of meanings, interpretations, definitions and disciplines ranging from psychology and philosophy to the highly commercialized Self-Help industry and Motivational sciences.

   a. AAAI
   b. A Stake in the Outcome
   c. Empowerment
   d. A4e

16. The _____ is the labour pool in employment. It is generally used to describe those working for a single company or industry, but can also apply to a geographic region like a city, country, state, etc. The term generally excludes the employers or management, and implies those involved in manual labour.
   a. Workforce
   b. Pink-collar worker
   c. Division of labour
   d. Work-life balance

17. An _____ is any party that makes an investment.

The term has taken on a specific meaning in finance to describe the particular types of people and companies that regularly purchase equity or debt securities for financial gain in exchange for funding an expanding company. Less frequently, the term is applied to parties who purchase real estate, currency, commodity derivatives, personal property, or other assets.

a. A Stake in the Outcome
b. A4e
c. AAAI
d. Investor

18. A mutual shareholder or _____ is an individual or company (including a corporation) that legally owns one or more shares of stock in a joint stock company. A company's shareholders collectively own that company. Thus, the typical goal of such companies is to enhance shareholder value.
   a. 1990 Clean Air Act
   b. Stockholder
   c. Shareholder
   d. Free riding

19. _____ refers to metrics and measures of output from production processes, per unit of input. Labor _____, for example, is typically measured as a ratio of output per labor-hour, an input. _____ may be conceived of as a metrics of the technical or engineering efficiency of production.
   a. Productivity
   b. Remanufacturing
   c. Value engineering
   d. Master production schedule

20. _____ is the concept of how effective an organization is in achieving the outcomes the organization intends to produce. The idea of _____ is especially important for non-profit organizations as most people who donate money to non-profit organizations and charities are interested in knowing whether the organization is effective in accomplishing its goals.

An organization's effectiveness is also dependent on its communicative competence and ethics.

   a. Organizational effectiveness
   b. Organizational development
   c. Informal organization
   d. Organizational structure

21. _____ is a family of standards for quality management systems. _____ is maintained by ISO, the International Organization for Standardization and is administered by accreditation and certification bodies. The rules are updated, the time and changes in the requirements for quality, motivate change.

a. ISO 9000
b. A Stake in the Outcome
c. AAAI
d. A4e

22. _____ is an integrated communications-based process through which individuals and communities discover that existing and newly-identified needs and wants may be satisfied by the products and services of others.

_____ is defined by the American _____ Association as the activity, set of institutions, and processes for creating, communicating, delivering, and exchanging offerings that have value for customers, clients, partners, and society at large. The term developed from the original meaning which referred literally to going to market, as in shopping, or going to a market to buy or sell goods or services.

a. Disruptive technology
b. Customer relationship management
c. Market development
d. Marketing

Chapter 3. Making Decisions

1. _____ can be regarded as an outcome of mental processes (cognitive process) leading to the selection of a course of action among several alternatives. Every _____ process produces a final choice. The output can be an action or an opinion of choice.
   a. 1990 Clean Air Act
   b. Decision making
   c. 33 Strategies of War
   d. 28-hour day

2. _____ consists of the mental process of thinking involved with the process of judging the merits of multiple options and selecting one of them for action. Some simple examples include deciding whether to get up in the morning or go back to sleep, or selecting a given route for a journey. More complex examples (often decisions that affect what a person thinks or their core beliefs) include choosing a lifestyle, religious affiliation, or political position.
   a. Championship mobilization
   b. Trade study
   c. Groups decision making
   d. Choice

3. In game theory, an _____ is a set of moves or strategies taken by the players, or their payoffs resulting from the actions or strategies taken by all players. The two are complementary in that given knowledge of the set of strategies of all players, the final state of the game is known, as are any relevant payoffs. In a game where chance or a random event is involved, the _____ is not known from only the set of strategies, but is only realized when the random event(s) are realized.
   a. A4e
   b. Outcome
   c. AAAI
   d. A Stake in the Outcome

4. In decision theory and estimation theory, the _____ of an estimator, $\hat{\theta}$, of an unknown parameter of the distribution, θ, is the expected value of the loss function

$$R(\theta, \hat{\theta}) = \mathbb{E}_\theta L(\theta, \hat{\theta}) = \int L(\theta, \hat{\theta})\, dP_\theta.$$

where dP_θ is a probability measure parametrized by θ.

- For a scalar parameter θ and a quadratic loss function,

$$L(\theta, \hat{\theta}) = (\theta - \hat{\theta})^2$$

the _____ function becomes the mean squared error of the estimate,

$$R(\theta, \hat{\theta}) = E_\theta (\theta - \hat{\theta})^2$$

- In density estimation, the unknown parameter is probability density itself. The loss function is typically chosen to be a norm in an appropriate function space. For example, for L^2 norm,

$$L(f, \hat{f}) = \|f - \hat{f}\|_2^2$$

the _____ function becomes the mean integrated squared error

$$R(f, \hat{f}) = E\|f - \hat{f}\|^2$$

a. Risk aversion
b. Financial modeling
c. Linear model
d. Risk

5. In probability theory and statistics, the _____ of a random variable is the integral of the random variable with respect to its probability measure. For discrete random variables this is equivalent to the probability-weighted sum of the possible values, and for continuous random variables with a density function it is the probability density -weighted integral of the possible values.
a. AAAI
b. Expected value
c. A Stake in the Outcome
d. A4e

6. In economics, business, retail, and accounting, a _____ is the value of money that has been used up to produce something, and hence is not available for use anymore. In economics, a _____ is an alternative that is given up as a result of a decision. In business, the _____ may be one of acquisition, in which case the amount of money expended to acquire it is counted as _____.

Chapter 3. Making Decisions

a. Fixed costs
b. Cost allocation
c. Cost overrun
d. Cost

7. _____ is a way of expressing knowledge or belief that an event will occur or has occurred. In mathematics the concept has been given an exact meaning in _____ theory, that is used extensively in such areas of study as mathematics, statistics, finance, gambling, science, and philosophy to draw conclusions about the likelihood of potential events and the underlying mechanics of complex systems.

The word _____ does not have a consistent direct definition.

a. Statistics
b. Probability
c. Standard deviation
d. Time series analysis

8. _____ is an advertisement in which a particular product specifically mentions a competitor by name for the express purpose of showing why the competitor is inferior to the product naming it.

This should not be confused with parody advertisements, where a fictional product is being advertised for the purpose of poking fun at the particular advertisement, nor should it be confused with the use of a coined brand name for the purpose of comparing the product without actually naming an actual competitor. ('Wikipedia tastes better and is less filling than the Encyclopedia Galactica.')

In the 1980s, during what has been referred to as the cola wars, soft-drink manufacturer Pepsi ran a series of advertisements where people, caught on hidden camera, in a blind taste test, chose Pepsi over rival Coca-Cola.

a. Comparative advertising
b. 28-hour day
c. 1990 Clean Air Act
d. 33 Strategies of War

9. In economics, _____ are business expenses that are not dependent on the activities of the business They tend to be time-related, such as salaries or rents being paid per month. This is in contrast to variable costs, which are volume-related (and are paid per quantity.)

In management accounting, _____ are defined as expenses that do not change in proportion to the activity of a business, within the relevant period or scale of production.

a. Transaction cost
b. Cost of quality
c. Cost allocation
d. Fixed costs

10. _____s are expenses that change in proportion to the activity of a business. In other words, _____ is the sum of marginal costs. It can also be considered normal costs.
   a. Fixed costs
   b. Cost overrun
   c. Cost accounting
   d. Variable cost

11. _____ of the learning curve effect and the closely related experience curve effect express the relationship between equations for experience and efficiency or between efficiency gains and investment in the effort. The experience of 'learning curves' was first observed by the 19th Century German psychologist Hermann Ebbinghaus according to the difficulty of memorizing varying numbers of verbal stimuli, and subsequent learning about the complex processes of learning are discussed in the

.

The rule used for representing the learning curve effect states that the more times a task has been performed, the less time will be required on each subsequent iteration.

   a. Spatial Decision Support Systems
   b. Point biserial correlation coefficient
   c. Models
   d. Distribution

12. In mathematics, _____ is a technique for optimization of a linear objective function, subject to linear equality and linear inequality constraints. Informally, _____ determines the way to achieve the best outcome (such as maximum profit or lowest cost) in a given mathematical model and given some list of requirements represented as linear equations.

More formally, given a polytope (for example, a polygon or a polyhedron), and a real-valued affine function

$$f(x_1, x_2, \ldots, x_n) = c_1 x_1 + c_2 x_2 + \cdots + c_n x_n + d$$

defined on this polytope, a _____ method will find a point in the polytope where this function has the smallest (or largest) value.

a. Linear programming relaxation
b. 1990 Clean Air Act
c. Slack variable
d. Linear programming

13. _____ is used to assign the available resources in an economic way. It is part of resource management.

In strategic planning, is a plan for using available resources, for example human resources, especially in the near term, to achieve goals for the future.

a. 33 Strategies of War
b. 1990 Clean Air Act
c. Resource allocation
d. 28-hour day

14. _____ is decision making in groups consisting of multiple members/entities. The challenge of group decision is deciding what action a group should take. There are various systems designed to solve this problem.
a. Control of Substances Hazardous to Health Regulations 2002
b. Genbutsu
c. Collaborative Planning, Forecasting and Replenishment
d. Groups decision making

15. _____ is a concept based on the fact that rationality of individuals is limited by the information they have, the cognitive limitations of their minds, and the finite amount of time they have to make decisions. This contrasts with the concept of rationality as optimization. Another way to look at _____ is that, because decision-makers lack the ability and resources to arrive at the optimal solution, they instead apply their rationality only after having greatly simplified the choices available.
a. Complete information
b. Transferable utility
c. Mixed strategy
d. Bounded rationality

16. The _____ captures an expanded spectrum of values and criteria for measuring organizational success: economic, ecological and social. With the ratification of the United Nations and ICLEI _____ standard for urban and community accounting in early 2007, this became the dominant approach to public sector full cost accounting. Similar UN standards apply to natural capital and human capital measurement to assist in measurements required by _____, e.g. the ecoBudget standard for reporting ecological footprint.

Chapter 3. Making Decisions

a. 33 Strategies of War
b. 1990 Clean Air Act
c. 28-hour day
d. Triple bottom line

17. _____ is an adjective for experience-based techniques that help in problem solving, learning and discovery. A _____ method is particularly used to rapidly come to a solution that is hoped to be close to the best possible answer, or 'optimal solution'. _____s are 'rules of thumb', educated guesses, intuitive judgments or simply common sense.
    a. Representativeness
    b. Heuristic
    c. 1990 Clean Air Act
    d. 28-hour day

18. The _____ is a phenomenon (which can result in a cognitive bias) in which people base their prediction of the frequency of an event or the proportion within a population based on how easily an example can be brought to mind.

Simply stated, where an anecdote ('I know an American guy who...') is used to 'prove' an entire proposition or to support a bias, the _____ is in play.

In these instances the ease of imagining an example or the vividness and emotional impact of that example becomes more credible than actual statistical probability.

   a. A Stake in the Outcome
   b. AAAI
   c. A4e
   d. Availability heuristic

19. _____ was first described by Barry M. Staw in his 1976 paper, 'Knee deep in the big muddy: A study of escalating commitment to a chosen course of action'. More recently the term Sunk cost fallacy has been used to describe the phenomenon where people justify increased investment in a decision, based on the cumulative prior investment, despite new evidence suggesting that the decision was probably wrong. Such investment may include money , time, or -- in the case of military strategy -- human lives.
   a. Open Options
   b. A4e
   c. A Stake in the Outcome
   d. Escalation of commitment

Chapter 3. Making Decisions

20. The _____ is a heuristic wherein people assume commonality between objects of similar appearance, or between an object and a group it appears to fit into. While often very useful in everyday life, it can also result in neglect of relevant base rates and other errors. The representative heuristic was first proposed by Amos Tversky and Daniel Kahneman.
   a. Representativeness heuristic
   b. 28-hour day
   c. Representativeness
   d. 1990 Clean Air Act

21. The 'business case for _____', theorizes that in a global marketplace, a company that employs a diverse workforce (both men and women, people of many generations, people from ethnically and racially diverse backgrounds etc.) is better able to understand the demographics of the marketplace it serves and is thus better equipped to thrive in that marketplace than a company that has a more limited range of employee demographics.

An additional corollary suggests that a company that supports the _____ of its workforce can also improve employee satisfaction, productivity and retention.

   a. Kanban
   b. Diversity
   c. Trademark
   d. Virtual team

22. In neuroscience, the _____ is a collection of brain structures which attempts to regulate and control behavior by inducing pleasurable effects.

A psychological reward is a process that reinforces behavior -- something that, when offered, causes a behavior to increase in intensity. Reward is an operational concept for describing the positive value an individual ascribes to an object, behavioral act or an internal physical state.

   a. 33 Strategies of War
   b. Reward system
   c. 1990 Clean Air Act
   d. 28-hour day

23. The _____ is the labour pool in employment. It is generally used to describe those working for a single company or industry, but can also apply to a geographic region like a city, country, state, etc. The term generally excludes the employers or management, and implies those involved in manual labour.

a. Division of labour
b. Pink-collar worker
c. Work-life balance
d. Workforce

Chapter 4. Monitoring the Environment

1. The _____ captures an expanded spectrum of values and criteria for measuring organizational success: economic, ecological and social. With the ratification of the United Nations and ICLEI _____ standard for urban and community accounting in early 2007, this became the dominant approach to public sector full cost accounting. Similar UN standards apply to natural capital and human capital measurement to assist in measurements required by _____, e.g. the ecoBudget standard for reporting ecological footprint.
    a. 33 Strategies of War
    b. 1990 Clean Air Act
    c. 28-hour day
    d. Triple bottom line

2. The _____ of 1990 (ADA) is the short title of United States (Pub.L. 101-336, 104 Stat. 327, enacted July 26, 1990), codified at 42 U.S.C. § 12101 et seq. It was signed into law on July 26, 1990, by President George H. W. Bush, and later amended with changes effective January 1, 2009. The ADA is a wide-ranging civil rights law that prohibits, under certain circumstances, discrimination based on disability. It affords similar protections against discrimination to Americans with disabilities as the Civil Rights Act of 1964,
    a. Americans with Disabilities Act
    b. Australian labour law
    c. Equal Pay Act of 1963
    d. Employment discrimination

3. The 'business case for _____', theorizes that in a global marketplace, a company that employs a diverse workforce (both men and women, people of many generations, people from ethnically and racially diverse backgrounds etc.) is better able to understand the demographics of the marketplace it serves and is thus better equipped to thrive in that marketplace than a company that has a more limited range of employee demographics.

An additional corollary suggests that a company that supports the _____ of its workforce can also improve employee satisfaction, productivity and retention.

   a. Virtual team
   b. Kanban
   c. Trademark
   d. Diversity

4. The _____ is the labour pool in employment. It is generally used to describe those working for a single company or industry, but can also apply to a geographic region like a city, country, state, etc. The term generally excludes the employers or management, and implies those involved in manual labour.

a. Pink-collar worker
b. Workforce
c. Division of labour
d. Work-life balance

5. A broad definition of _____ is the action of gathering, analyzing, and distributing information about products, customers, competitors and any aspect of the environment needed to support executives and managers in making strategic decisions for an organization.

Key points of this definitions:

1. _____ is an ethical and legal business practice. (This is important as _____ professionals emphasize that the discipline is not the same as industrial espionage which is both unethical and usually illegal.)
2. The focus is on the external business environment.
3. There is a process involved in gathering information, converting it into intelligence and then utilizing this in business decision making. _____ professionals emphasize that if the intelligence gathered is not usable (or actionable) then it is not intelligence.

A more focused definition of _____ regards it as the organizational function responsible for the early identification of risks and opportunities in the market before they become obvious. Experts also call this process the early signal analysis. This definition focuses attention on the difference between dissemination of widely available factual information (such as market statistics, financial reports, newspaper clippings) performed by functions such as libraries and information centers, and _____ which is a perspective on developments and events aimed at yielding a competitive edge.

a. Competitor or Competitive Intelligence
b. 28-hour day
c. 1990 Clean Air Act
d. Competitive intelligence

6. _____ is a process of gathering, analyzing, and dispensing information for tactical or strategic purposes. The _____ process entails obtaining both factual and subjective information on the business environments in which a company is operating or considering entering.

Chapter 4. Monitoring the Environment

There are three ways of scanning the business environment:

- Ad-hoc scanning - Short term, infrequent examinations usually initiated by a crisis
- Regular scanning - Studies done on a regular schedule (say, once a year)
- Continuous scanning(also called continuous learning) - continuous structured data collection and processing on a broad range of environmental factors

Most commentators feel that in today's turbulent business environment the best scanning method available is continuous scanning. This allows the firm to :

-act quickly-take advantage of opportunities before competitors do-respond to environmental threats before significant damage is done

   a. A Stake in the Outcome
   b. Environmental scanning
   c. AAAI
   d. A4e

7. The term '_____' refers to the concept of collecting information and attempting to spot a pattern in the information. In some fields of study, the term '_____' has more formally-defined meanings.

In project management _____ is a mathematical technique that uses historical results to predict future outcome.

   a. Trend analysis
   b. Stepwise regression
   c. Regression analysis
   d. Least squares

8. _____ is the process of estimation in unknown situations. Prediction is a similar, but more general term. Both can refer to estimation of time series, cross-sectional or longitudinal data.
   a. 1990 Clean Air Act
   b. 28-hour day
   c. 33 Strategies of War
   d. Forecasting

9. In game theory, an _____ is a set of moves or strategies taken by the players, or their payoffs resulting from the actions or strategies taken by all players. The two are complementary in that given knowledge of the set of strategies of all players, the final state of the game is known, as are any relevant payoffs. In a game where chance or a random event is involved, the _____ is not known from only the set of strategies, but is only realized when the random event(s) are realized.
   a. AAAI
   b. A Stake in the Outcome
   c. A4e
   d. Outcome

10. _____ is the process of comparing the cost, cycle time, productivity, or quality of a specific process or method to another that is widely considered to be an industry standard or best practice. Essentially, _____ provides a snapshot of the performance of your business and helps you understand where you are in relation to a particular standard. The result is often a business case for making changes in order to make improvements.
    a. Complementors
    b. Cost leadership
    c. Competitive heterogeneity
    d. Benchmarking

11. _____ is a business management strategy aimed at embedding awareness of quality in all organizational processes. _____ has been widely used in manufacturing, education, hospitals, call centers, government, and service industries, as well as NASA space and science programs.

As defined by the International Organization for Standardization (ISO):

> '_____ is a management approach for an organization, centered on quality, based on the participation of all its members and aiming at long-term success through customer satisfaction, and benefits to all members of the organization and to society.' ISO 8402:1994

One major aim is to reduce variation from every process so that greater consistency of effort is obtained. (Royse, D., Thyer, B., Padgett D., ' Logan T., 2006)

   a. Total quality management
   b. 28-hour day
   c. Quality management
   d. 1990 Clean Air Act

Chapter 4. Monitoring the Environment

12. _____ is a process or productivity improvement tool intended to have a stable and consistent growth and improvement of all the segments of a process or processes. _____ ensures the process stabilization and further improvement. When an organization's growth and development is intended, identification of all the processes and development of a measurement analysis of each process step is necessary.
    a. 33 Strategies of War
    b. 28-hour day
    c. 1990 Clean Air Act
    d. Continual improvement

13. _____ can be considered to have three main components: quality control, quality assurance and quality improvement. _____ is focused not only on product quality, but also the means to achieve it. _____ therefore uses quality assurance and control of processes as well as products to achieve more consistent quality.
    a. Total quality management
    b. 28-hour day
    c. 1990 Clean Air Act
    d. Quality management

14. _____ refers to the process of screening, and selecting qualified people for a job at an organization or firm mid- and large-size organizations and companies often retain professional recruiters or outsource some of the process to _____ agencies. External _____ is the process of attracting and selecting employees from outside the organization.

The _____ industry has four main types of agencies: employment agencies, _____ websites and job search engines, 'headhunters' for executive and professional _____, and in-house _____.

   a. Referral recruitment
   b. Recruitment Process Outsourcing
   c. Recruitment
   d. Labour hire

15. In statistics and image processing, to smooth a data set is to create an approximating function that attempts to capture important patterns in the data, while leaving out noise or other fine-scale structures/rapid phenomena. Many different algorithms are used in _____. One of the most common algorithms is the 'moving average', often used to try to capture important trends in repeated statistical surveys.
    a. 1990 Clean Air Act
    b. 28-hour day
    c. 33 Strategies of War
    d. Smoothing

16. In decision theory and estimation theory, the _____ of an estimator, $\hat{\theta}$, of an unknown parameter of the distribution, θ, is the expected value of the loss function

$$R(\theta, \hat{\theta}) = \mathbb{E}_\theta L(\theta, \hat{\theta}) = \int L(\theta, \hat{\theta}) \, dP_\theta.$$

where dP_θ is a probability measure parametrized by θ.

- For a scalar parameter θ and a quadratic loss function,

$$L(\theta, \hat{\theta}) = (\theta - \hat{\theta})^2$$

the _____ function becomes the mean squared error of the estimate,

$$R(\theta, \hat{\theta}) = E_\theta(\theta - \hat{\theta})^2$$

- In density estimation, the unknown parameter is probability density itself. The loss function is typically chosen to be a norm in an appropriate function space. For example, for L^2 norm,

$$L(f, \hat{f}) = \|f - \hat{f}\|_2^2$$

the _____ function becomes the mean integrated squared error

$$R(f, \hat{f}) = E\|f - \hat{f}\|^2$$

a. Risk
b. Risk aversion
c. Linear model
d. Financial modeling

17. _____ is a form of communication that typically attempts to persuade potential customers to purchase or to consume more of a particular brand of product or service. 'While now central to the contemporary global economy and the reproduction of global production networks, it is only quite recently that _____ has been more than a marginal influence on patterns of sales and production. The formation of modern _____ was intimately bound up with the emergence of new forms of monopoly capitalism around the end of the 19th and beginning of the 20th century as one element in corporate strategies to create, organize and where possible control markets, especially for mass produced consumer goods.

a. A Stake in the Outcome
b. A4e
c. AAAI
d. Advertising

18. _____ in its literal sense is the process of transformation of local or regional phenomena into global ones. It can be described as a process by which the people of the world are unified into a single society and function together.

This process is a combination of economic, technological, sociocultural and political forces.

a. Globalization
b. Collaborative Planning, Forecasting and Replenishment
c. Histogram
d. Cost Management

19. A _____ is a process in which a potential employee is evaluated by an employer for prospective employment in their company, organization and was established in the late 16th century.

A _____ typically precedes the hiring decision, and is used to evaluate the candidate. The interview is usually preceded by the evaluation of submitted résumés from interested candidates, then selecting a small number of candidates for interviews.

a. Split shift
b. Job interview
c. Supported employment
d. Payrolling

20. _____ is a family of standards for quality management systems. _____ is maintained by ISO, the International Organization for Standardization and is administered by accreditation and certification bodies. The rules are updated, the time and changes in the requirements for quality, motivate change.
a. A Stake in the Outcome
b. ISO 9000
c. AAAI
d. A4e

21. The _____, widely known as ISO , is an international-standard-setting body composed of representatives from various national standards organizations. Founded on 23 February 1947, the organization promulgates worldwide proprietary industrial and commercial standards. It is headquartered in Geneva, Switzerland.

a. A Stake in the Outcome
b. AAAI
c. A4e
d. International Organization for Standardization

Chapter 5. Planning Systems

1. A _____ is a brief written statement of the purpose of a company or organization. Ideally, a _____ guides the actions of the organization, spells out its overall goal, provides a sense of direction, and guides decision making for all levels of management.

   _____s often contain the following:

   - Purpose and aim of the organization
   - The organization's primary stakeholders: clients, stockholders, etc.
   - Responsibilities of the organization toward these stakeholders
   - Products and services offered

   In developing a _____:

   - Encourage as much input as feasible from employees, volunteers, and other stakeholders
   - Publicize it broadly

   The _____ can be used to resolve differences between business stakeholders. Stakeholders include: employees including managers and executives, stockholders, board of directors, customers, suppliers, distributors, creditors, governments (local, state, federal, etc.), unions, competitors, NGO's, and the general public.

   a. 28-hour day
   b. 1990 Clean Air Act
   c. 33 Strategies of War
   d. Mission statement

2. The _____ captures an expanded spectrum of values and criteria for measuring organizational success: economic, ecological and social. With the ratification of the United Nations and ICLEI _____ standard for urban and community accounting in early 2007, this became the dominant approach to public sector full cost accounting. Similar UN standards apply to natural capital and human capital measurement to assist in measurements required by _____, e.g. the ecoBudget standard for reporting ecological footprint.
   a. 1990 Clean Air Act
   b. 33 Strategies of War
   c. 28-hour day
   d. Triple bottom line

3. _____ is a strategic planning method used to evaluate the Strengths, Weaknesses, Opportunities, and Threats involved in a project or in a business venture. It involves specifying the objective of the business venture or project and identifying the internal and external factors that are favorable and unfavorable to achieving that objective. The technique is credited to Albert Humphrey, who led a convention at Stanford University in the 1960s and 1970s using data from Fortune 500 companies.

a. Marketing
b. Market share
c. Corporate image
d. SWOT analysis

4. _____ is, in very basic words, a position a firm occupies against its competitors.

According to Michael Porter, the three methods for creating a sustainable _____ are through:

1. Cost leadership

2. Differentiation

3. Focus (economics)

   a. 28-hour day
   b. 1990 Clean Air Act
   c. Theory Z
   d. Competitive advantage

5. In economics, business, retail, and accounting, a _____ is the value of money that has been used up to produce something, and hence is not available for use anymore. In economics, a _____ is an alternative that is given up as a result of a decision. In business, the _____ may be one of acquisition, in which case the amount of money expended to acquire it is counted as _____.
   a. Cost
   b. Cost allocation
   c. Cost overrun
   d. Fixed costs

6. _____ is one of the managerial functions like planning, organizing, staffing and directing. It is an important function because it helps to check the errors and to take the corrective action so that deviation from standards are minimized and stated goals of the organization are achieved in desired manner. According to modern concepts, _____ is a foreseeing action whereas earlier concept of _____ was used only when errors were detected. _____ in management means setting standards, measuring actual performance and taking corrective action.
   a. Turnover
   b. Decision tree pruning
   c. Schedule of reinforcement
   d. Control

7. _____ refers to the movement of cash into or out of a business or financial product. It is usually measured during a specified, finite period of time. Measurement of _____ can be used

- to determine a project's rate of return or value. The time of _____s into and out of projects are used as inputs in financial models such as internal rate of return, and net present value.
- to determine problems with a business's liquidity. Being profitable does not necessarily mean being liquid. A company can fail because of a shortage of cash, even while profitable.
- as an alternate measure of a business's profits when it is believed that accrual accounting concepts do not represent economic realities. For example, a company may be notionally profitable but generating little operational cash (as may be the case for a company that barters its products rather than selling for cash.) In such a case, the company may be deriving additional operating cash by issuing shares evaluating default risk, re-investment requirements, etc.

_____ is a generic term used differently depending on the context. It may be defined by users for their own purposes.

a. Gross profit margin
b. Sweat equity
c. Gross profit
d. Cash flow

8. _____ is the discipline of planning, organizing and managing resources to bring about the successful completion of specific project goals and objectives. It is often closely related to and sometimes conflated with Program management.

A project is a finite endeavor--having specific start and completion dates--undertaken to meet particular goals and objectives, usually to bring about beneficial change or added value.

a. Project engineer
b. Work package
c. Precedence diagram
d. Project management

9. _____ generally refers to a list of all planned expenses and revenues. It is a plan for saving and spending. A _____ is an important concept in microeconomics, which uses a _____ line to illustrate the trade-offs between two or more goods.
a. 33 Strategies of War
b. 1990 Clean Air Act
c. 28-hour day
d. Budget

10. _____ according to Onuoha (2007) is the practice of starting new organizations or revitalizing mature organizations, particularly new businesses generally in response to identified opportunities. _____ is often a difficult undertaking, as a vast majority of new businesses fail. Entrepreneurial activities are substantially different depending on the type of organization that is being started.

   a. A4e
   b. AAAI
   c. A Stake in the Outcome
   d. Entrepreneurship

11. In decision theory and estimation theory, the _____ of an estimator, $\hat{\theta}$, of an unknown parameter of the distribution, θ, is the expected value of the loss function

$$R(\theta, \hat{\theta}) = \mathbb{E}_\theta L(\theta, \hat{\theta}) = \int L(\theta, \hat{\theta})\, dP_\theta.$$

where dP_θ is a probability measure parametrized by θ.

- For a scalar parameter θ and a quadratic loss function,

$$L(\theta, \hat{\theta}) = (\theta - \hat{\theta})^2$$

   the _____ function becomes the mean squared error of the estimate,

$$R(\theta, \hat{\theta}) = E_\theta (\theta - \hat{\theta})^2$$

- In density estimation, the unknown parameter is probability density itself. The loss function is typically chosen to be a norm in an appropriate function space. For example, for L^2 norm,

$$L(f, \hat{f}) = \|f - \hat{f}\|_2^2$$

   the _____ function becomes the mean integrated squared error

$$R(f, \hat{f}) = E\|f - \hat{f}\|^2$$

a. Risk aversion
b. Financial modeling
c. Linear model
d. Risk

12. An _____ is a person who has possession of an enterprise and assumes significant accountability for the inherent risks and the outcome. It is an ambitious leader who combines land, labor, and capital to create and market new goods or services. The term is a loanword from French and was first defined by the Irish economist Richard Cantillon.
    a. AAAI
    b. A Stake in the Outcome
    c. A4e
    d. Entrepreneur

13. _____ is the practice of using entrepreneurial skills without taking on the risks or accountability associated with entrepreneurial activities. It is practiced by employees within an established organization using a business model. Employees, perhaps engaged in a special project within a larger firm are supposed to behave as entrepreneurs, even though they have the resources and capabilities of the larger firm to draw upon.
    a. Intrapreneurship
    b. A4e
    c. AAAI
    d. A Stake in the Outcome

14. In game theory, an _____ is a set of moves or strategies taken by the players, or their payoffs resulting from the actions or strategies taken by all players. The two are complementary in that given knowledge of the set of strategies of all players, the final state of the game is known, as are any relevant payoffs. In a game where chance or a random event is involved, the _____ is not known from only the set of strategies, but is only realized when the random event(s) are realized.
    a. Outcome
    b. A Stake in the Outcome
    c. AAAI
    d. A4e

15. _____ is a civil designation for persons who are incorporated in a fixed or permanent way to a society or group: regular member of the working staff, permanent staff distinguished from a supernumerary.

The term '_____' and its counterpart, 'supernumerary,' originated in Spanish and Latin American academy and government; it is now also used in countries all over the world, such as France, the U.S., England, Italy, etc.

There are _____ members of surgical organizations, of universities, of gastronomical associations, etc.

a. Affiliation
b. Adam Smith
c. Abraham Harold Maslow
d. Numerary

16. _____ has become one of the most popular theories in organizational psychology.

Goal setting has been a formula used for acheivement since the early 1800s. The form and pattern has cahanged drastically over the years and there is still much debate as to what is the most efective pattern to follow.

a. Human relations
b. Job satisfaction
c. Corporate Culture
d. Goal-setting theory

17. _____ describes the situation when output from (or information about the result of) an event or phenomenon in the past will influence the same event/phenomenon in the present or future. When an event is part of a chain of cause-and-effect that forms a circuit or loop, then the event is said to 'feed back' into itself.

_____ is also a synonym for:

- _____ signal; the information about the initial event that is the basis for subsequent modification of the event.
- _____ loop; the causal path that leads from the initial generation of the _____ signal to the subsequent modification of the event.

_____ is a mechanism, process or signal that is looped back to control a system within itself. Such a loop is called a _____ loop.

a. Positive feedback
b. 1990 Clean Air Act
c. Feedback
d. Feedback loop

18. _____ is a process of agreeing upon objectives within an organization so that management and employees agree to the objectives and understand what they are in the organization.

Chapter 5. Planning Systems

The term '_____' was first popularized by Peter Drucker in his 1954 book 'The Practice of Management'.

The essence of _____ is participative goal setting, choosing course of actions and decision making.

    a. Management by Objectives
    b. Job enrichment
    c. Clean sheet review
    d. Business economics

19. _____ can be regarded as an outcome of mental processes (cognitive process) leading to the selection of a course of action among several alternatives. Every _____ process produces a final choice. The output can be an action or an opinion of choice.
    a. 33 Strategies of War
    b. 1990 Clean Air Act
    c. 28-hour day
    d. Decision making

20. _____ refers to a range of skills, tools, and techniques used to manage time when accomplishing specific tasks, projects and goals. This set encompass a wide scope of activities, and these include planning, allocating, setting goals, delegation, analysis of time spent, monitoring, organizing, scheduling, and prioritizing. Initially _____ referred to just business or work activities, but eventually the term broadened to include personal activities also.
    a. Voice of the customer
    b. Time management
    c. Cash cow
    d. Formula for Change

21. In economics, _____ is the desire to own something and the ability to pay for it. The term _____ signifies the ability or the willingness to buy a particular commodity at a given point of time.
    a. 1990 Clean Air Act
    b. 33 Strategies of War
    c. 28-hour day
    d. Demand

Chapter 6. Monitoring Performance Through Control Systems   41

1. _____ is one of the managerial functions like planning, organizing, staffing and directing. It is an important function because it helps to check the errors and to take the corrective action so that deviation from standards are minimized and stated goals of the organization are achieved in desired manner. According to modern concepts, _____ is a foreseeing action whereas earlier concept of _____ was used only when errors were detected. _____ in management means setting standards, measuring actual performance and taking corrective action.
   a. Decision tree pruning
   b. Schedule of reinforcement
   c. Turnover
   d. Control

2. A _____ is a change implemented to address a weakness identified in a management system. Normally _____s are implemented in response to a customer complaint, abnormal levels of internal nonconformity, nonconformities identified during an internal audit or adverse or unstable trends in product and process monitoring such as would be identified by SPC.

   The process of determining a _____ requires identification of actions that can be taken to prevent or mitigate the weakness.

   a. Zero defects
   b. 28-hour day
   c. Corrective action
   d. 1990 Clean Air Act

3. There are two types of _____ relationships: formal and informal. Informal relationships develop on their own between partners. Formal _____, on the other hand, refers to assigned relationships, often associated with organizational _____ programs designed to promote employee development or to assist at-risk children and youth.
   a. Mentoring
   b. Human resource management system
   c. Real Property Administrator
   d. Fix it twice

4. In organizational development (OD), _____ is the application of Socio-Technical Systems principles and techniques to the humanization of work.

   The aims of _____ to improved job satisfaction, to improved through-put, to improved quality and to reduced employee problems, e.g., grievances, absenteeism.

   Under scientific management people would be directed by reason and the problems of industrial unrest would be appropriately (i.e., scientifically) addressed.

a. Path-goal theory
b. Management process
c. Work design
d. Graduate recruitment

5. _____ generally refers to a list of all planned expenses and revenues. It is a plan for saving and spending. A _____ is an important concept in microeconomics, which uses a _____ line to illustrate the trade-offs between two or more goods.
   a. Budget
   b. 28-hour day
   c. 1990 Clean Air Act
   d. 33 Strategies of War

6. _____ is a method by which the job performance of an employee is evaluated _____ is a part of career development.

_____s are regular reviews of employee performance within organizations

Generally, the aims of a _____ are to:

- Give feedback on performance to employees.
- Identify employee training needs.
- Document criteria used to allocate organizational rewards.
- Form a basis for personnel decisions: salary increases, promotions, disciplinary actions, etc.
- Provide the opportunity for organizational diagnosis and development.
- Facilitate communication between employee and administraton
- Validate selection techniques and human resource policies to meet federal Equal Employment Opportunity requirements.

A common approach to assessing performance is to use a numerical or scalar rating system whereby managers are asked to score an individual against a number of objectives/attributes. In some companies, employees receive assessments from their manager, peers, subordinates and customers while also performing a self assessment.

   a. Personnel management
   b. Performance appraisal
   c. Progressive discipline
   d. Human resource management

Chapter 6. Monitoring Performance Through Control Systems

7. In neuroscience, the _____ is a collection of brain structures which attempts to regulate and control behavior by inducing pleasurable effects.

A psychological reward is a process that reinforces behavior -- something that, when offered, causes a behavior to increase in intensity. Reward is an operational concept for describing the positive value an individual ascribes to an object, behavioral act or an internal physical state.

a. 28-hour day
b. 33 Strategies of War
c. 1990 Clean Air Act
d. Reward system

8. _____ can be regarded as an outcome of mental processes (cognitive process) leading to the selection of a course of action among several alternatives. Every _____ process produces a final choice. The output can be an action or an opinion of choice.
a. 1990 Clean Air Act
b. 33 Strategies of War
c. Decision making
d. 28-hour day

9. The general definition of an _____ is an evaluation of a person, organization, system, process, project or product. _____s are performed to ascertain the validity and reliability of information; also to provide an assessment of a system's internal control. The goal of an _____ is to express an opinion on the person / organization/system (etc) in question, under evaluation based on work done on a test basis.
a. Audit committee
b. A Stake in the Outcome
c. Audit
d. Internal control

10. In finance, a _____ or accounting ratio is a ratio of two selected numerical values taken from an enterprise's financial statements. There are many standard ratios used to try to evaluate the overall financial condition of a corporation or other organization. _____s may be used by managers within a firm, by current and potential shareholders (owners) of a firm, and by a firm's creditors.
a. Financial ratio
b. Rate of return
c. Return on sales
d. Return on equity

Chapter 6. Monitoring Performance Through Control Systems

11. _____ are formal records of the financial activities of a business, person, or other entity. In British English, including United Kingdom company law, _____ are often referred to as accounts, although the term _____ is also used, particularly by accountants.

_____ provide an overview of a business or person's financial condition in both short and long term.

a. 33 Strategies of War
b. 1990 Clean Air Act
c. Financial statements
d. 28-hour day

12. A _____ is a type of bar chart that illustrates a project schedule. _____s illustrate the start and finish dates of the terminal elements and summary elements of a project. Terminal elements and summary elements comprise the work breakdown structure of the project.

a. 1990 Clean Air Act
b. 28-hour day
c. 33 Strategies of War
d. Gantt chart

13. _____ is the level of inventory that minimizes the total inventory holding costs and ordering costs. The framework used to determine this order quantity is also known as Wilson _____ Model. The model was developed by F. W. Harris in 1913.

a. Economic order quantity
b. Anti-leadership
c. Effective executive
d. Event management

14. In economics, business, retail, and accounting, a _____ is the value of money that has been used up to produce something, and hence is not available for use anymore. In economics, a _____ is an alternative that is given up as a result of a decision. In business, the _____ may be one of acquisition, in which case the amount of money expended to acquire it is counted as _____.

a. Cost allocation
b. Cost
c. Cost overrun
d. Fixed costs

Chapter 6. Monitoring Performance Through Control Systems 45

15. A _____ is a subset of the overall internal controls of a business covering the application of people, documents, technologies, and procedures by management accountants to solving business problems such as costing a product, service or a business-wide strategy. _____s are distinct from regular information systems in that they are used to analyze other information systems applied in operational activities in the organization. Academically, the term is commonly used to refer to the group of information management methods tied to the automation or support of human decision making, e.g. Decision Support Systems, Expert systems, and Executive information systems.
   a. 28-hour day
   b. Management information system
   c. Strategic information system
   d. 1990 Clean Air Act

16. _____, e-commuting, e-work, telework, working from home (WFH), or working at home (WAH) is a work arrangement in which employees enjoy flexibility in working location and hours. In other words, the daily commute to a central place of work is replaced by telecommunication links. Many work from home, while others, occasionally also referred to as nomad workers or web commuters utilize mobile telecommunications technology to work from coffee shops or myriad other locations.
   a. 28-hour day
   b. 1990 Clean Air Act
   c. Telecommuting
   d. 33 Strategies of War

17. _____ is an advertisement in which a particular product specifically mentions a competitor by name for the express purpose of showing why the competitor is inferior to the product naming it.

This should not be confused with parody advertisements, where a fictional product is being advertised for the purpose of poking fun at the particular advertisement, nor should it be confused with the use of a coined brand name for the purpose of comparing the product without actually naming an actual competitor. ('Wikipedia tastes better and is less filling than the Encyclopedia Galactica.')

In the 1980s, during what has been referred to as the cola wars, soft-drink manufacturer Pepsi ran a series of advertisements where people, caught on hidden camera, in a blind taste test, chose Pepsi over rival Coca-Cola.

   a. 28-hour day
   b. 1990 Clean Air Act
   c. 33 Strategies of War
   d. Comparative advertising

18. The Program (or Project) Evaluation and Review Technique, commonly abbreviated _____, is a model for project management designed to analyze and represent the tasks involved in completing a given project.

_____ is a method to analyze the involved tasks in completing a given project, specially the time needed to complete each task, and identifying the minimum time needed to complete the total project.

_____ was developed primarily to simplify the planning and scheduling of large and complex projects.

a. 33 Strategies of War
b. 28-hour day
c. 1990 Clean Air Act
d. PERT

19. _____ refers to the movement of cash into or out of a business or financial product. It is usually measured during a specified, finite period of time. Measurement of _____ can be used

- to determine a project's rate of return or value. The time of _____s into and out of projects are used as inputs in financial models such as internal rate of return, and net present value.
- to determine problems with a business's liquidity. Being profitable does not necessarily mean being liquid. A company can fail because of a shortage of cash, even while profitable.
- as an alternate measure of a business's profits when it is believed that accrual accounting concepts do not represent economic realities. For example, a company may be notionally profitable but generating little operational cash (as may be the case for a company that barters its products rather than selling for cash.) In such a case, the company may be deriving additional operating cash by issuing shares evaluating default risk, re-investment requirements, etc.

_____ is a generic term used differently depending on the context. It may be defined by users for their own purposes.

a. Gross profit margin
b. Cash flow
c. Gross profit
d. Sweat equity

20. _____ is a way of expressing knowledge or belief that an event will occur or has occurred. In mathematics the concept has been given an exact meaning in _____ theory, that is used extensively in such areas of study as mathematics, statistics, finance, gambling, science, and philosophy to draw conclusions about the likelihood of potential events and the underlying mechanics of complex systems.

The word _____ does not have a consistent direct definition.

a. Standard deviation
b. Statistics
c. Time series analysis
d. Probability

21. In probability theory, a probability distribution is called _____ if its cumulative distribution function is _____. This is equivalent to saying that for random variables X with the distribution in question, Pr[X = a] = 0 for all real numbers a, i.e.: the probability that X attains the value a is zero, for any number a. If the distribution of X is _____ then X is called a _____ random variable.
   a. Continuous
   b. Connectionist expert systems
   c. Decision tree pruning
   d. Pay Band

22. In probability theory, the _____ states conditions under which the sum of a sufficiently large number of independent random variables, each with finite mean and variance, will be approximately normally distributed. Since real-world quantities are often the balanced sum of many unobserved random events, this theorem provides a partial explanation for the prevalence of the normal probability distribution. The _____ also justifies the approximation of large-sample statistics to the normal distribution in controlled experiments.
   a. Heavy-tailed distributions
   b. Pay Band
   c. Point biserial correlation coefficient
   d. Central limit theorem

23. In probability theory and statistics, the _____ or Gaussian distribution is a continuous probability distribution that describes data that clusters around a mean or average. The graph of the associated probability density function is bell-shaped, with a peak at the mean, and is known as the Gaussian function or bell curve.

The _____ can be used to describe, at least approximately, any variable that tends to cluster around the mean.

   a. Generalized normal distribution
   b. Histogram
   c. Heteroskedastic
   d. Normal distribution

Chapter 6. Monitoring Performance Through Control Systems

24. In probability theory and statistics, _____ is a measure of the variability or dispersion of a population, a data set, or a probability distribution. A low _____ indicates that the data points tend to be very close to the same value (the mean), while high _____ indicates that the data are 'spread out' over a large range of values.

For example, the average height for adult men in the United States is about 70 inches (178 cm), with a _____ of around 3 in (8 cm.)

   a. Failure rate
   b. Frequency distribution
   c. Normal distribution
   d. Standard deviation

25. _____ is one of the four elements of marketing mix. An organization or set of organizations (go-betweens) involved in the process of making a product or service available for use or consumption by a consumer or business user.

The other three parts of the marketing mix are product, pricing, and promotion.

   a. Missing completely at random
   b. Matching theory
   c. Job creation programs
   d. Distribution

26. _____ is an integrated communications-based process through which individuals and communities discover that existing and newly-identified needs and wants may be satisfied by the products and services of others.

_____ is defined by the American _____ Association as the activity, set of institutions, and processes for creating, communicating, delivering, and exchanging offerings that have value for customers, clients, partners, and society at large. The term developed from the original meaning which referred literally to going to market, as in shopping, or going to a market to buy or sell goods or services.

   a. Market development
   b. Customer relationship management
   c. Disruptive technology
   d. Marketing

Chapter 7. Technology and the Design of Work Processes

1. _____ refers to metrics and measures of output from production processes, per unit of input. Labor _____, for example, is typically measured as a ratio of output per labor-hour, an input. _____ may be conceived of as a metrics of the technical or engineering efficiency of production.
   a. Master production schedule
   b. Value engineering
   c. Remanufacturing
   d. Productivity

2. _____ is an inventory strategy that strives to improve the return on investment of a business by reducing in-process inventory and its associated carrying costs. To meet _____ objectives, the process relies on signals between different points in the process. This means the process is often driven by a series of signals, or Kanban, which tell production when to make the next part. Kanban are usually 'tickets' but can be simple visual signals, such as the presence or absence of a part on a shelf. Implemented correctly, _____ can dramatically improve a manufacturing organization's return on investment, quality, and efficiency.
   a. 28-hour day
   b. 33 Strategies of War
   c. 1990 Clean Air Act
   d. Just-in-time

3. _____ is a concept related to lean and just-in-time (JIT) production. The Japanese word _____ is a common term meaning 'signboard' or 'billboard'. According to Taiichi Ohno, the man credited with developing JIT, _____ is a means through which JIT is achieved.
   a. Risk management
   b. Succession planning
   c. Trademark
   d. Kanban

4. A _____ is a list of the general tasks and responsibilities of a position. Typically, it also includes to whom the position reports, specifications such as the qualifications needed by the person in the job, salary range for the position, etc. A _____ is usually developed by conducting a job analysis, which includes examining the tasks and sequences of tasks necessary to perform the job.
   a. Recruitment
   b. Recruitment advertising
   c. Job description
   d. Recruitment Process Insourcing

5. A _____ system is a manufacturing system in which there is some amount of flexibility that allows the system to react in the case of changes, whether predicted or unpredicted. This flexibility is generally considered to fall into two categories, which both contain numerous subcategories.

Chapter 7. Technology and the Design of Work Processes

The first category, machine flexibility, covers the system's ability to be changed to produce new product types, and ability to change the order of operations executed on a part. The second category is called routing flexibility, which consists of the ability to use multiple machines to perform the same operation on a part, as well as the system's ability to absorb large-scale changes, such as in volume, capacity, or capability.

a. Manufacturing resource planning
b. Flexible manufacturing
c. Jidoka
d. Homeworkers

6. _____ is the production of large amounts of standardized products, including and especially on assembly lines. The concepts of _____ are applied to various kinds of products, from fluids and particulates handled in bulk to discrete solid parts to assemblies of such parts

_____ of assemblies typically uses electric-motor-powered moving tracks or conveyor belts to move partially complete products to workers, who perform simple repetitive tasks.

a. 28-hour day
b. 1990 Clean Air Act
c. 33 Strategies of War
d. Mass production

7. _____ is an advertisement in which a particular product specifically mentions a competitor by name for the express purpose of showing why the competitor is inferior to the product naming it.

This should not be confused with parody advertisements, where a fictional product is being advertised for the purpose of poking fun at the particular advertisement, nor should it be confused with the use of a coined brand name for the purpose of comparing the product without actually naming an actual competitor. ('Wikipedia tastes better and is less filling than the Encyclopedia Galactica.')

In the 1980s, during what has been referred to as the cola wars, soft-drink manufacturer Pepsi ran a series of advertisements where people, caught on hidden camera, in a blind taste test, chose Pepsi over rival Coca-Cola.

a. 1990 Clean Air Act
b. 28-hour day
c. 33 Strategies of War
d. Comparative advertising

Chapter 7. Technology and the Design of Work Processes

8. _____ is one of the four elements of marketing mix. An organization or set of organizations (go-betweens) involved in the process of making a product or service available for use or consumption by a consumer or business user.

The other three parts of the marketing mix are product, pricing, and promotion.

a. Distribution
b. Missing completely at random
c. Job creation programs
d. Matching theory

9. _____ are long-format television commercials, typically five minutes or longer.. _____ are also known as paid programming (or teleshopping in Europe.) Originally, they were a phenomenon that started in the United States where they were typically shown overnight (usually 2:00 a.m. to 6:00 a.m.)

a. A Stake in the Outcome
b. AAAI
c. A4e
d. Infomercials

10. In probability theory, a probability distribution is called _____ if its cumulative distribution function is _____. This is equivalent to saying that for random variables X with the distribution in question, Pr[X = a] = 0 for all real numbers a, i.e.: the probability that X attains the value a is zero, for any number a. If the distribution of X is _____ then X is called a _____ random variable.

a. Connectionist expert systems
b. Continuous
c. Decision tree pruning
d. Pay Band

11. _____ is a management process whereby delivery (customer valued) processes are constantly evaluated and improved in the light of their efficiency, effectiveness and flexibility.

Some see it as a meta process for most management systems (Business Process Management, Quality Management, Project Management). Deming saw it as part of the 'system' whereby feedback from the process and customer were evaluated against organisational goals.

a. Continuous Improvement Process
b. Critical Success Factor
c. Sole proprietorship
d. First-mover advantage

Chapter 7. Technology and the Design of Work Processes

12. _____ ('Plan-Do-Check-Act') is an iterative four-step problem-solving process typically used in business process improvement. It is also known as the Deming Cycle, Shewhart cycle, Deming Wheel, or Plan-Do-Study-Act.

_____ was made popular by Dr. W. Edwards Deming, who is considered by many to be the father of modern quality control; however it was always referred to by him as the Shewhart cycle. Later in Deming's career, he modified _____ to Plan, Do, Study, Act (PDSA) so as to better describe his recommendations.

a. Decentralization
b. Management team
c. Management by exception
d. PDCA

13. _____ is an integrated communications-based process through which individuals and communities discover that existing and newly-identified needs and wants may be satisfied by the products and services of others.

_____ is defined by the American _____ Association as the activity, set of institutions, and processes for creating, communicating, delivering, and exchanging offerings that have value for customers, clients, partners, and society at large. The term developed from the original meaning which referred literally to going to market, as in shopping, or going to a market to buy or sell goods or services.

a. Market development
b. Marketing
c. Customer relationship management
d. Disruptive technology

14. _____ is a family of standards for quality management systems. _____ is maintained by ISO, the International Organization for Standardization and is administered by accreditation and certification bodies. The rules are updated, the time and changes in the requirements for quality, motivate change.
a. A Stake in the Outcome
b. AAAI
c. ISO 9000
d. A4e

15. _____ is a business management strategy aimed at embedding awareness of quality in all organizational processes. _____ has been widely used in manufacturing, education, hospitals, call centers, government, and service industries, as well as NASA space and science programs.

Chapter 7. Technology and the Design of Work Processes 53

As defined by the International Organization for Standardization (ISO):

'_____ is a management approach for an organization, centered on quality, based on the participation of all its members and aiming at long-term success through customer satisfaction, and benefits to all members of the organization and to society.' ISO 8402:1994

One major aim is to reduce variation from every process so that greater consistency of effort is obtained. (Royse, D., Thyer, B., Padgett D., ' Logan T., 2006)

a. 28-hour day
b. Quality management
c. 1990 Clean Air Act
d. Total quality management

16. _____ is a process or productivity improvement tool intended to have a stable and consistent growth and improvement of all the segments of a process or processes. _____ ensures the process stabilization and further improvement. When an organization's growth and development is intended, identification of all the processes and development of a measurement analysis of each process step is necessary.

a. Continual improvement
b. 1990 Clean Air Act
c. 33 Strategies of War
d. 28-hour day

17. _____ can be considered to have three main components: quality control, quality assurance and quality improvement. _____ is focused not only on product quality, but also the means to achieve it. _____ therefore uses quality assurance and control of processes as well as products to achieve more consistent quality.

a. Quality management
b. 1990 Clean Air Act
c. Total quality management
d. 28-hour day

18.

_____ is a systematic method to improve the 'value' of goods or products and services by using an examination of function. Value, as defined, is the ratio of function to cost. Value can therefore be increased by either improving the function or reducing the cost.

Chapter 7. Technology and the Design of Work Processes

a. Value engineering
b. Master production schedule
c. Capacity planning
d. Cellular manufacturing

19. _____ is the use of control systems (such as numerical control, programmable logic control, and other industrial control systems), in concert with other applications of information technology (such as computer-aided technologies [CAD, CAM, CAx]), to control industrial machinery and processes, reducing the need for human intervention. In the scope of industrialization, _____ is a step beyond mechanization. Whereas mechanization provided human operators with machinery to assist them with the physical requirements of work, _____ greatly reduces the need for human sensory and mental requirements as well.
    a. AAAI
    b. Automation
    c. A Stake in the Outcome
    d. A4e

20. A _____ is a depiction of a sequence of operations, declared as work of a person, a group of persons, an organization of staff, or one or more simple or complex mechanisms. _____ may be seen as any abstraction of real work, segregated in workshare, work split or other types of ordering. For control purposes, _____ may be a view on real work under a chosen aspect, thus serving as a virtual representation of actual work.
    a. Resource-based view
    b. Management development
    c. Time management
    d. Workflow

21. _____ can be regarded as an outcome of mental processes (cognitive process) leading to the selection of a course of action among several alternatives. Every _____ process produces a final choice. The output can be an action or an opinion of choice.
    a. 1990 Clean Air Act
    b. 28-hour day
    c. Decision making
    d. 33 Strategies of War

Chapter 7. Technology and the Design of Work Processes

22. An _____ is software that attempts to reproduce the performance of one or more human experts, most commonly in a specific problem domain, and is a traditional application and/or subfield of artificial intelligence. A wide variety of methods can be used to simulate the performance of the expert however common to most or all are 1) the creation of a so-called 'knowledgebase' which uses some knowledge representation formalism to capture the Subject Matter Experts (SME) knowledge and 2) a process of gathering that knowledge from the SME and codifying it according to the formalism, which is called knowledge engineering. _____s may or may not have learning components but a third common element is that once the system is developed it is proven by being placed in the same real world problem solving situation as the human SME, typically as an aid to human workers or a supplement to some information system.

    a. A4e
    b. A Stake in the Outcome
    c. AAAI
    d. Expert system

23. _____ is the process of sharing of skills, knowledge, technologies, methods of manufacturing, samples of manufacturing and facilities among governments and other institutions to ensure that scientific and technological developments are accessible to a wider range of users who can then further develop and exploit the technology into new products, processes, applications, materials or services. It is closely related to (and may arguably be considered a subset of) Knowledge transfer. Related terms, used almost synonymously, include 'technology valorisation' and 'technology commercialisation'.

    a. Mediation
    b. Technology transfer
    c. Competition law
    d. Munn v. Illinois

24. _____ is the state of being which occurs when a person, object, or service is no longer wanted even though it may still be in good working order. _____ frequently occurs because a replacement has become available that is superior in one or more aspects. Videotapes making way for DVDs

Technical _____ may occur when a new product or technology supersedes the old, and it becomes preferred to utilize the new technology in place of the old.

    a. AAAI
    b. A Stake in the Outcome
    c. Obsolescence
    d. A4e

25. In organizational development (OD), _____ is the application of Socio-Technical Systems principles and techniques to the humanization of work.

The aims of _____ to improved job satisfaction, to improved through-put, to improved quality and to reduced employee problems, e.g., grievances, absenteeism.

Under scientific management people would be directed by reason and the problems of industrial unrest would be appropriately (i.e., scientifically) addressed.

a. Management process
b. Graduate recruitment
c. Path-goal theory
d. Work design

26. In game theory, an _____ is a set of moves or strategies taken by the players, or their payoffs resulting from the actions or strategies taken by all players. The two are complementary in that given knowledge of the set of strategies of all players, the final state of the game is known, as are any relevant payoffs. In a game where chance or a random event is involved, the _____ is not known from only the set of strategies, but is only realized when the random event(s) are realized.
a. A Stake in the Outcome
b. AAAI
c. A4e
d. Outcome

27. _____ is an attempt to motivate employees by giving them the opportunity to use the range of their abilities. It is an idea that was developed by the American psychologist Frederick Herzberg in the 1950s. It can be contrasted to job enlargement which simply increases the number of tasks without changing the challenge.
a. Cash cow
b. Catfish effect
c. C-A-K-E
d. Job enrichment

28. _____ describes the situation when output from (or information about the result of) an event or phenomenon in the past will influence the same event/phenomenon in the present or future. When an event is part of a chain of cause-and-effect that forms a circuit or loop, then the event is said to 'feed back' into itself.

Chapter 7. Technology and the Design of Work Processes 57

_____ is also a synonym for:

- _____ signal; the information about the initial event that is the basis for subsequent modification of the event.
- _____ loop; the causal path that leads from the initial generation of the _____ signal to the subsequent modification of the event.

_____ is a mechanism, process or signal that is looped back to control a system within itself. Such a loop is called a _____ loop.

a. Feedback
b. Feedback loop
c. 1990 Clean Air Act
d. Positive feedback

29. _____ is the change (processing) of information in any manner detectable by an observer. As such, it is a process which describes everything which happens (changes) in the universe, from the falling of a rock (a change in position) to the printing of a text file from a digital computer system. In the latter case, an information processor is changing the form of presentation of that text file.

a. AAAI
b. Information processing
c. A Stake in the Outcome
d. A4e

30. The 'business case for _____', theorizes that in a global marketplace, a company that employs a diverse workforce (both men and women, people of many generations, people from ethnically and racially diverse backgrounds etc.) is better able to understand the demographics of the marketplace it serves and is thus better equipped to thrive in that marketplace than a company that has a more limited range of employee demographics.

An additional corollary suggests that a company that supports the _____ of its workforce can also improve employee satisfaction, productivity and retention.

a. Trademark
b. Kanban
c. Diversity
d. Virtual team

Chapter 7. Technology and the Design of Work Processes

31. _____ is a variable work schedule, in contrast to traditional work arrangements requiring employees to work a standard 9am to 5pm day. Under _____, there is typically a core period of the day when employees are expected to be at work (for example, between 11 am and 3pm), while the rest of the working day is 'flexitime', in which employees can choose when they work, subject to achieving total daily, weekly or monthly hours in the region of what the employer expects, and subject to the necessary work being done.

A _____ policy allows staff to determine when they will work, while a flexplace policy allows staff to determine where they will work.

   a. Fiduciary
   b. Bennett Amendment
   c. Certificate of Incorporation
   d. Flextime

32. In finance, an _____ is a contract between a buyer and a seller that gives the buyer the right--but not the obligation--to buy or to sell a particular asset (the underlying asset) at a later day at an agreed price. In return for granting the _____, the seller collects a payment (the premium) from the buyer. A call _____ gives the buyer the right to buy the underlying asset; a put _____ gives the buyer of the _____ the right to sell the underlying asset.
   a. A4e
   b. A Stake in the Outcome
   c. AAAI
   d. Option

33. The _____ is the labour pool in employment. It is generally used to describe those working for a single company or industry, but can also apply to a geographic region like a city, country, state, etc. The term generally excludes the employers or management, and implies those involved in manual labour.
   a. Workforce
   b. Pink-collar worker
   c. Work-life balance
   d. Division of labour

34. _____, e-commuting, e-work, telework, working from home (WFH), or working at home (WAH) is a work arrangement in which employees enjoy flexibility in working location and hours. In other words, the daily commute to a central place of work is replaced by telecommunication links. Many work from home, while others, occasionally also referred to as nomad workers or web commuters utilize mobile telecommunications technology to work from coffee shops or myriad other locations.

a. 28-hour day
b. 33 Strategies of War
c. 1990 Clean Air Act
d. Telecommuting

Chapter 8. Organization Design

1. The _____ captures an expanded spectrum of values and criteria for measuring organizational success: economic, ecological and social. With the ratification of the United Nations and ICLEI _____ standard for urban and community accounting in early 2007, this became the dominant approach to public sector full cost accounting. Similar UN standards apply to natural capital and human capital measurement to assist in measurements required by _____, e.g. the ecoBudget standard for reporting ecological footprint.
    a. 1990 Clean Air Act
    b. 28-hour day
    c. 33 Strategies of War
    d. Triple bottom line

2. _____ refers to the process of grouping activities into departments.

   Division of labour creates specialists who need coordination. This coordination is facilitated by grouping specialists together in departments.

    a. Decent work
    b. Maximum wage
    c. Division of labour
    d. Departmentalization

3. In a military context, the _____ is the line of authority and responsibility along which orders are passed within a military unit and between different units. The term is also used in a civilian management context describing comparable hierarchical structures of authority.
    a. 1990 Clean Air Act
    b. 28-hour day
    c. Chain of command
    d. French leave

4. The _____ is a standardized, on-scene, all-hazard incident management concept. It is a management protocol originally designed for emergency management agencies in the United States which was later federalized there. It has since been adopted by agencies in other countries.
    a. AAAI
    b. A Stake in the Outcome
    c. A4e
    d. Incident Command Structure

5. _____ is a term originating in military organization theory, but now used more commonly in business management, particularly human resource management. _____ refers to the number of subordinates a supervisor has.

Chapter 8. Organization Design

In the hierarchical business organization of the past it was not uncommon to see average spans of 1 to 10 or even less. That is, one manager supervised ten employees on average.

a. Span of control
b. Mentoring
c. Senior management
d. CIFMS

6. _____ is one of the managerial functions like planning, organizing, staffing and directing. It is an important function because it helps to check the errors and to take the corrective action so that deviation from standards are minimized and stated goals of the organization are achieved in desired manner.According to modern concepts, _____ is a foreseeing action whereas earlier concept of _____ was used only when errors were detected. _____ in management means setting standards, measuring actual performance and taking corrective action.
   a. Decision tree pruning
   b. Turnover
   c. Schedule of reinforcement
   d. Control

7. _____ is the process by which the activities of an organisation, particularly those regarding decision-making, become concentrated within a particular location and/or group.
   a. Chief operating officer
   b. Corner office
   c. Product innovation
   d. Centralization

8. _____ is the process of dispersing decision-making governance closer to the people or citizen. It includes the dispersal of administration or governance in sectors or areas like engineering, management science, political science, political economy, sociology and economics. _____ is also possible in the dispersal of population and employment.
   a. Business plan
   b. Frenemy
   c. Decentralization
   d. Formula for Change

9. In economics, business, retail, and accounting, a _____ is the value of money that has been used up to produce something, and hence is not available for use anymore. In economics, a _____ is an alternative that is given up as a result of a decision. In business, the _____ may be one of acquisition, in which case the amount of money expended to acquire it is counted as _____.

a. Cost allocation
b. Fixed costs
c. Cost overrun
d. Cost

10. _____ is an integrated communications-based process through which individuals and communities discover that existing and newly-identified needs and wants may be satisfied by the products and services of others.

_____ is defined by the American _____ Association as the activity, set of institutions, and processes for creating, communicating, delivering, and exchanging offerings that have value for customers, clients, partners, and society at large. The term developed from the original meaning which referred literally to going to market, as in shopping, or going to a market to buy or sell goods or services.

a. Market development
b. Disruptive technology
c. Customer relationship management
d. Marketing

11. In finance, an _____ is a contract between a buyer and a seller that gives the buyer the right--but not the obligation-- to buy or to sell a particular asset (the underlying asset) at a later day at an agreed price. In return for granting the _____, the seller collects a payment (the premium) from the buyer. A call _____ gives the buyer the right to buy the underlying asset; a put _____ gives the buyer of the _____ the right to sell the underlying asset.

a. A4e
b. A Stake in the Outcome
c. AAAI
d. Option

12. _____ can be regarded as an outcome of mental processes (cognitive process) leading to the selection of a course of action among several alternatives. Every _____ process produces a final choice. The output can be an action or an opinion of choice.

a. 28-hour day
b. 33 Strategies of War
c. 1990 Clean Air Act
d. Decision making

13. _____, in marketing, manufacturing, call centres and management, is the use of flexible computer-aided manufacturing systems to produce custom output. Those systems combine the low unit costs of mass production processes with the flexibility of individual customization.

Chapter 8. Organization Design

'_____' is the new frontier in business competition for both manufacturing and service industries.

a. 1990 Clean Air Act
b. 28-hour day
c. 33 Strategies of War
d. Mass customization

14. _____ refers to the movement of cash into or out of a business or financial product. It is usually measured during a specified, finite period of time. Measurement of _____ can be used

- to determine a project's rate of return or value. The time of _____s into and out of projects are used as inputs in financial models such as internal rate of return, and net present value.
- to determine problems with a business's liquidity. Being profitable does not necessarily mean being liquid. A company can fail because of a shortage of cash, even while profitable.
- as an alternate measure of a business's profits when it is believed that accrual accounting concepts do not represent economic realities. For example, a company may be notionally profitable but generating little operational cash (as may be the case for a company that barters its products rather than selling for cash.) In such a case, the company may be deriving additional operating cash by issuing shares evaluating default risk, re-investment requirements, etc.

_____ is a generic term used differently depending on the context. It may be defined by users for their own purposes.

a. Sweat equity
b. Gross profit margin
c. Gross profit
d. Cash flow

15. _____ is 'interfirm coordination that is characterized by organic or informal social systems, in contrast to bureaucratic structures within firms and formal contractual relationships between them.(Gerlach, 1992:64; Nohria, 1992)' A useful survey of network organization theory appears in Van Alstyne (1997).

The concepts of privatization, public private partnership, and contracting are defined in this context.

As a concept, _____ explains increased efficiency and reduced agency problems for organizations existing in highly turbulent environments . Due to the rapid pace of modern society and competitive pressures from globalization, _____ has gained prominence and development among sociological theorists. As a concept, _____ explains increased efficiency and reduced agency problems for organizations existing in highly turbulent environments.

a. 1990 Clean Air Act
b. Network governance
c. 33 Strategies of War
d. 28-hour day

16. A _____ is a list of the general tasks and responsibilities of a position. Typically, it also includes to whom the position reports, specifications such as the qualifications needed by the person in the job, salary range for the position, etc. A _____ is usually developed by conducting a job analysis, which includes examining the tasks and sequences of tasks necessary to perform the job.
   a. Recruitment Process Insourcing
   b. Recruitment
   c. Job description
   d. Recruitment advertising

17. _____ is subcontracting a process, such as product design or manufacturing, to a third-party company. The decision to outsource is often made in the interest of lowering cost or making better use of time and energy costs, redirecting or conserving energy directed at the competencies of a particular business, or to make more efficient use of land, labor, capital, (information) technology and resources. _____ became part of the business lexicon during the 1980s.
   a. Operant conditioning
   b. Unemployment insurance
   c. Opinion leadership
   d. Outsourcing

18. A _____ is a contemporary apporach to organizational design. It is an organization that is not defined by, or limited to, the horizontal, vertical, or external boundaries imposed by a predefined structure. This term was coined by former GE chairman Jack Welch because he wanted to eliminate vertical and horizontal boundaries within GE and break down external barriers between the company and its customers and suppliers.
   a. Business Roundtable
   b. Headquarters
   c. Boundaryless organization
   d. Chief risk officer

Chapter 9. Managing Human Resources

1. _____ is the strategic and coherent approach to the management of an organisation's most valued assets - the people working there who individually and collectively contribute to the achievement of the objectives of the business. The terms '_____' and 'human resources' (HR) have largely replaced the term 'personnel management' as a description of the processes involved in managing people in organizations. In simple sense, _____ means employing people, developing their resources, utilizing, maintaining and compensating their services in tune with the job and organizational requirement.
    a. Revolving door syndrome
    b. Progressive discipline
    c. Job knowledge
    d. Human resource management

2. _____ is a process of planning and controlling the performance or execution of any type of activity, such as:

    - a project (project _____) or
    - a process (process _____, sometimes referred to as the process performance measurement and management system.)

    Organization's senior management is responsible for carrying out its _____.

    a. Management process
    b. Participatory management
    c. Work design
    d. Human Relations Movement

3. The _____ of 1990 (ADA) is the short title of United States (Pub.L. 101-336, 104 Stat. 327, enacted July 26, 1990), codified at 42 U.S.C. § 12101 et seq. It was signed into law on July 26, 1990, by President George H. W. Bush, and later amended with changes effective January 1, 2009. The ADA is a wide-ranging civil rights law that prohibits, under certain circumstances, discrimination based on disability. It affords similar protections against discrimination to Americans with disabilities as the Civil Rights Act of 1964,
    a. Equal Pay Act of 1963
    b. Australian labour law
    c. Employment discrimination
    d. Americans with Disabilities Act

4. The 'business case for _____', theorizes that in a global marketplace, a company that employs a diverse workforce (both men and women, people of many generations, people from ethnically and racially diverse backgrounds etc.) is better able to understand the demographics of the marketplace it serves and is thus better equipped to thrive in that marketplace than a company that has a more limited range of employee demographics.

An additional corollary suggests that a company that supports the _____ of its workforce can also improve employee satisfaction, productivity and retention.

a. Trademark
b. Virtual team
c. Kanban
d. Diversity

5. The _____ 1970 is an Act of the United Kingdom Parliament which prohibits any less favourable treatment between men and women in terms of pay and conditions of employment. It came into force on 29 December 1975. The term pay is interpreted in a broad sense to include, on top of wages, things like holidays, pension rights, company perks and some kinds of bonuses.

   a. Oncale v. Sundowner Offshore Services
   b. Australian labour law
   c. Equal Pay Act
   d. Architectural Barriers Act of 1968

6. The field of _____ looks at the relationship between management and workers, particularly groups of workers represented by a union.

   _____ is an important factor in analyzing 'varieties of capitalism', such as neocorporatism, social democracy, and neoliberalism

   a. Industrial relations
   b. Overtime
   c. Organizational effectiveness
   d. Informal organization

7. The _____ is a 1935 United States federal law that limits the means with which employers may react to workers in the private sector that organize labor unions, engage in collective bargaining, and take part in strikes and other forms of concerted activity in support of their demands. The Act does not, on the other hand, cover those workers who are covered by the Railway Labor Act, agricultural employees, domestic employees, supervisors, independent contractors and some close relatives of individual employers.

   It was in a context of severe economic troubles that the Wagner Act came into effect.

   a. 28-hour day
   b. 1990 Clean Air Act
   c. 33 Strategies of War
   d. National Labor Relations Act

Chapter 9. Managing Human Resources 67

8. _____ is an increasingly broadening term with which an organization, or other human system describes the combination of traditionally administrative personnel functions with acquisition and application of skills, knowledge and experience, Employee Relations and resource planning at various levels. The field draws upon concepts developed in Industrial/Organizational Psychology and System Theory. _____ has at least two related interpretations depending on context. The original usage derives from political economy and economics, where it was traditionally called labor, one of four factors of production although this perspective is changing as a function of new and ongoing research into more strategic approaches at national levels. This first usage is used more in terms of '_____ development', and can go beyond just organizations to the level of nations . The more traditional usage within corporations and businesses refers to the individuals within a firm or agency, and to the portion of the organization that deals with hiring, firing, training, and other personnel issues, typically referred to as `_____ management'.
 a. Bradford Factor
 b. Human resources
 c. Human resource management
 d. Progressive discipline

9. The _____ is the labour pool in employment. It is generally used to describe those working for a single company or industry, but can also apply to a geographic region like a city, country, state, etc. The term generally excludes the employers or management, and implies those involved in manual labour.
 a. Work-life balance
 b. Workforce
 c. Division of labour
 d. Pink-collar worker

10. The _____ of 1967, Pub. L. No. 90-202, 81 Stat. 602 (Dec. 15, 1967), codified as Chapter 14 of Title 29 of the United States Code, 29 U.S.C. Â§ 621 through 29 U.S.C. Â§ 634 (ADEA), prohibits employment discrimination against persons 40 years of age or older in the United States). The law also sets standards for pensions and benefits provided by employers and requires that information about the needs of older workers be provided to the general public.
 a. Age Discrimination in Employment Act
 b. Extra time
 c. Unemployment and Farm Relief Act
 d. Undue hardship

11. _____ is one of the managerial functions like planning, organizing, staffing and directing. It is an important function because it helps to check the errors and to take the corrective action so that deviation from standards are minimized and stated goals of the organization are achieved in desired manner.According to modern concepts, _____ is a foreseeing action whereas earlier concept of _____ was used only when errors were detected. _____ in management means setting standards, measuring actual performance and taking corrective action.

a. Schedule of reinforcement
b. Turnover
c. Control
d. Decision tree pruning

12. The U.S. _____ of 1988 ('_____') generally prevents employers from using lie detector tests, either for pre-employment screening or during the course of employment, with certain exemptions. Employers generally may not require or request any employee or job applicant to take a lie detector test, or discharge, discipline, or discriminate against an employee or job applicant for refusing to take a test or for exercising other rights under the Act. In addition, employers are required to display a poster in the workplace explaining the _____ for their employees.
    a. AAAI
    b. A4e
    c. Employee Polygraph Protection Act
    d. A Stake in the Outcome

13. _____ is a contract between two parties, one being the employer and the other being the employee. An employee may be defined as: 'A person in the service of another under any contract of hire, express or implied, oral or written, where the employer has the power or right to control and direct the employee in the material details of how the work is to be performed.' Black's Law Dictionary page 471 (5th ed. 1979.)
    a. Employment
    b. Employment counsellor
    c. Exit interview
    d. Employment rate

14. The term _____ was created by President Lyndon B. Johnson when he signed Executive Order 11246 on September 24, 1965, created to prohibit federal contractors from discriminating against employees on the basis of race, sex, creed, religion, color, or national origin. In more recent times, most employers have also added sexual orientation to the list of non-discrimination.

The Executive Order also required contractors to implement affirmative action plans to increase the participation of minorities and women in the workplace.

    a. Equal Employment Opportunity
    b. A4e
    c. AAAI
    d. A Stake in the Outcome

Chapter 9. Managing Human Resources 69

15. The U.S. _____ is a federal agency whose goal is ending employment discrimination. The _____ investigates discrimination complaints based on an individual's race, color, national origin, religion, sex, age, disability and retaliation for reporting and/or opposing a discriminatory practice. The Commission is also tasked with filing suits on behalf of alleged victim(s) of discrimination against employers and as an adjudicatory for claims of discrimination brought against federal agencies.
   a. ARCO
   b. Airbus Industrie
   c. Airbus SAS
   d. Equal Employment Opportunity Commission

16. The _____ is a United States labor law allowing an employee to take unpaid leave due to a serious health condition that makes the employee unable to perform his job or to care for a sick family member or to care for a new son or daughter (including by birth, adoption or foster care.) The bill was among the first signed into law by President Bill Clinton in his first term.
   a. Contributory negligence
   b. Family and Medical Leave Act of 1993
   c. Harvester Judgment
   d. Sarbanes-Oxley Act of 2002

17. _____ is a cross-disciplinary area concerned with protecting the safety, health and welfare of people engaged in work or employment. The goal of all _____ programs is to foster a work free safe environment. As a secondary effect, it may also protect co-workers, family members, employers, customers, suppliers, nearby communities, and other members of the public who are impacted by the workplace environment.
   a. A Stake in the Outcome
   b. A4e
   c. Occupational Safety and Health
   d. AAAI

18. The _____ is the primary federal law which governs occupational health and safety in the private sector and federal government in the United States. It was enacted by Congress in 1970 and was signed by President Richard Nixon on December 29, 1970. Its main goal is to ensure that employers provide employees with an environment free from recognized hazards, such as exposure to toxic chemicals, excessive noise levels, mechanical dangers, heat or cold stress, or unsanitary conditions.
   a. Occupational Safety and Health Act
   b. Unemployment and Farm Relief Act
   c. Unemployment Action Center
   d. United States Department of Justice

Chapter 9. Managing Human Resources

19. _____ occurs when expectant women are fired, not hired, or otherwise discriminated against due to their pregnancy or intention to become pregnant. Common forms of _____ include not being hired due to visible pregnancy or likelihood of becoming pregnant, being fired after informing an employer of one's pregnancy, being fired after maternity leave, and receiving a pay dock due to pregnancy. In the United States, since 1978, employers are legally bound to provide what insurance, leave pay, and additional support that would be bestowed upon any employee with medical leave or disability.
    a. 28-hour day
    b. 33 Strategies of War
    c. Pregnancy Discrimination
    d. 1990 Clean Air Act

20. The U.S. _____ of 1973 prohibits discrimination on the basis of disability in programs conducted by Federal agencies, in programs receiving Federal financial assistance, in Federal employment, and in the employment practices of Federal contractors. The standards for determining employment discrimination under the _____ are the same as those used in title I of the Americans with Disabilities Act.

There are four key sections of the Act.

    a. 33 Strategies of War
    b. 1990 Clean Air Act
    c. 28-hour day
    d. Rehabilitation Act

21. _____ is the point where a person stops employment completely. A person may also semi-retire and keep some sort of _____ job, out of choice rather than necessity. This usually happens upon reaching a determined age, when physical conditions don't allow the person to work any more (by illness or accident), or even for personal choice (usually in the presence of an adequate pension or personal savings.)
    a. Termination of employment
    b. Wrongful dismissal
    c. Severance package
    d. Retirement

22. _____ is the process of learning a new skill or trade, often in response to a change in the economic environment. Generally it reflects changes in profession choice rather than an 'upward' movement in the same field.

There is some controversy surrounding the use of _____ to offset economic changes caused by free trade and automation.

Chapter 9. Managing Human Resources

a. Compliance Training
b. Suspension training
c. Krauthammer
d. Retraining

23. The _____ is a United States labor law which protects employees, their families, and communities by requiring most employers with 100 or more employees to provide sixty- (60) calendar-day advance notification of plant closings and mass layoffs of employees. It was enacted in 1989.

Employees entitled to notice under the _____ include managers and supervisors, hourly wage, and salaried workers.

a. Robinson-Patman Act
b. Leave of absence
c. Non-disclosure agreement
d. Worker Adjustment and Retraining Notification Act

24.

The terms _____ and positive action refer to policies that take race, ethnicity, or gender into consideration in an attempt to promote equal opportunity. The focus of such policies ranges from employment and education to public contracting and health programs. The impetus towards _____ is twofold: to maximize diversity in all levels of society, along with its presumed benefits, and to redress perceived disadvantages due to overt, institutional, or involuntary discrimination.

a. Abraham Harold Maslow
b. Affiliation
c. Adam Smith
d. Affirmative Action

25. _____ is the body of laws, administrative rulings, and precedents which address the legal rights of, and restrictions on, working people and their organizations. As such, it mediates many aspects of the relationship between trade unions, employers and employees. In Canada, employment laws related to unionized workplaces are differentiated from those relating to particular individuals.

a. Four-day week
b. Shift work
c. Trade union
d. Labor Law

Chapter 9. Managing Human Resources

26. _____ a term coined in the mid-20th century, refers to the belief or attitude that one gender or sex is inferior to, less competent, or less valuable than the other. It can also refer to hatred of, or prejudice towards, either sex as a whole , or the application of stereotypes of masculinity in relation to men, or of femininity in relation to women. It is also called male and female chauvinism.
   a. Reverse discrimination
   b. Separate but equal
   c. 1990 Clean Air Act
   d. Sexism,

27. The _____ 1975 is an Act of the Parliament of the United Kingdom to protect men and women from discrimination on the grounds of sex. The Act is mainly in relation to employment, training, education, harassment, the provision of goods and services and in the disposal of premises. The Gender Recognition Act 2004 and the The _____ 1975 (Amendment) Regulations 2008, amended parts of this Act to apply to transgender people.
   a. Sex Discrimination Act
   b. 1990 Clean Air Act
   c. 28-hour day
   d. 33 Strategies of War

28. A _____ is a body of elected or appointed members who jointly oversee the activities of a company or organization. The body sometimes has a different name, such as board of trustees, board of governors, board of managers, or executive board. It is often simply referred to as 'the board.'

A board's activities are determined by the powers, duties, and responsibilities delegated to it or conferred on it by an authority outside itself.

   a. Board of directors
   b. Competition law
   c. Foreign Corrupt Practices Act
   d. Clean Water Act

29. _____ can be regarded as an outcome of mental processes (cognitive process) leading to the selection of a course of action among several alternatives. Every _____ process produces a final choice. The output can be an action or an opinion of choice.
   a. 33 Strategies of War
   b. 28-hour day
   c. Decision making
   d. 1990 Clean Air Act

Chapter 9. Managing Human Resources

30. _____ refers to various methodologies for analyzing the requirements of a job.

The general purpose of _____ is to document the requirements of a job and the work performed. Job and task analysis is performed as a basis for later improvements, including: definition of a job domain; describing a job; developing performance appraisals, selection systems, promotion criteria, training needs assessment, and compensation plans.

 a. Hersey-Blanchard situational theory
 b. Management process
 c. Work design
 d. Job analysis

31. A _____ is a list of the general tasks and responsibilities of a position. Typically, it also includes to whom the position reports, specifications such as the qualifications needed by the person in the job, salary range for the position, etc. A _____ is usually developed by conducting a job analysis, which includes examining the tasks and sequences of tasks necessary to perform the job.
 a. Job description
 b. Recruitment
 c. Recruitment advertising
 d. Recruitment Process Insourcing

32. The _____ captures an expanded spectrum of values and criteria for measuring organizational success: economic, ecological and social. With the ratification of the United Nations and ICLEI _____ standard for urban and community accounting in early 2007, this became the dominant approach to public sector full cost accounting. Similar UN standards apply to natural capital and human capital measurement to assist in measurements required by _____, e.g. the ecoBudget standard for reporting ecological footprint.
 a. 28-hour day
 b. 33 Strategies of War
 c. 1990 Clean Air Act
 d. Triple bottom line

33. _____ refers to the process of screening, and selecting qualified people for a job at an organization or firm mid- and large-size organizations and companies often retain professional recruiters or outsource some of the process to _____ agencies. External _____ is the process of attracting and selecting employees from outside the organization.

The _____ industry has four main types of agencies: employment agencies, _____ websites and job search engines, 'headhunters' for executive and professional _____, and in-house _____.

a. Referral recruitment
b. Recruitment
c. Labour hire
d. Recruitment Process Outsourcing

34. The term _____ in logic applies to arguments or statements.

An argument is valid if and only if the truth of its premises entails the truth of its conclusion, it would be self-contradictory to affirm the premises and deny the conclusion. The corresponding conditional of a valid argument is a logical truth and the negation of its corresponding conditional is a contradiction.

a. Fuzzy logic
b. Simplification
c. 1990 Clean Air Act
d. Validity

35. _____ is a process of gathering, analyzing, and dispensing information for tactical or strategic purposes. The _____ process entails obtaining both factual and subjective information on the business environments in which a company is operating or considering entering.

There are three ways of scanning the business environment:

- Ad-hoc scanning - Short term, infrequent examinations usually initiated by a crisis
- Regular scanning - Studies done on a regular schedule (say, once a year)
- Continuous scanning(also called continuous learning) - continuous structured data collection and processing on a broad range of environmental factors

Most commentators feel that in today's turbulent business environment the best scanning method available is continuous scanning. This allows the firm to :

-act quickly-take advantage of opportunities before competitors do-respond to environmental threats before significant damage is done

a. A Stake in the Outcome
b. AAAI
c. A4e
d. Environmental scanning

36.

Chapter 9. Managing Human Resources

_____ is a commonly used, yet poorly defined concept in industrial and organizational psychology, the branch of psychology that deals with the workplace. It most commonly refers to whether a person performs their job well. Despite the confusion over how it should be exactly defined, performance is an extremely important criterion that relates to organizational outcomes and success.

a. 1990 Clean Air Act
b. 28-hour day
c. 33 Strategies of War
d. Job performance

37. '_____' refers to mental and communicative algorithms applied during social communications and interactions in order to reach certain effects or results. The term '_____' is used often in business contexts to refer to the measure of a person's ability to operate within business organizations through social communication and interactions. _____ are how people relate to one another.
a. A Stake in the Outcome
b. A4e
c. Interpersonal skills
d. AAAI

38. _____ is a system of training a new generation of practitioners of a skill. Apprentices (or in early modern usage 'prentices') or prot>ég>és build their careers from _____s. Most of their training is done on the job while working for an employer who helps the apprentices learn their trade, in exchange for their continuing labour for an agreed period after they become skilled.
a. A Stake in the Outcome
b. AAAI
c. A4e
d. Apprenticeship

39. _____ is an approach to management development where an individual is moved through a schedule of assignments designed to give him or her a breadth of exposure to the entire operation.

_____ is also practiced to allow qualified employees to gain more insights into the processes of a company, and to reduce boredom and increase job satisfaction through job variation.

The term _____ can also mean the scheduled exchange of persons in offices, especially in public offices, prior to the end of incumbency or the legislative period.

Chapter 9. Managing Human Resources

a. 1990 Clean Air Act
b. 33 Strategies of War
c. Job rotation
d. 28-hour day

40. _____ is a method by which the job performance of an employee is evaluated _____ is a part of career development.

_____s are regular reviews of employee performance within organizations

Generally, the aims of a _____ are to:

- Give feedback on performance to employees.
- Identify employee training needs.
- Document criteria used to allocate organizational rewards.
- Form a basis for personnel decisions: salary increases, promotions, disciplinary actions, etc.
- Provide the opportunity for organizational diagnosis and development.
- Facilitate communication between employee and administraton
- Validate selection techniques and human resource policies to meet federal Equal Employment Opportunity requirements.

A common approach to assessing performance is to use a numerical or scalar rating system whereby managers are asked to score an individual against a number of objectives/attributes. In some companies, employees receive assessments from their manager, peers, subordinates and customers while also performing a self assessment.

a. Personnel management
b. Progressive discipline
c. Performance appraisal
d. Human resource management

41. In game theory, an _____ is a set of moves or strategies taken by the players, or their payoffs resulting from the actions or strategies taken by all players. The two are complementary in that given knowledge of the set of strategies of all players, the final state of the game is known, as are any relevant payoffs. In a game where chance or a random event is involved, the _____ is not known from only the set of strategies, but is only realized when the random event(s) are realized.
a. A Stake in the Outcome
b. A4e
c. AAAI
d. Outcome

Chapter 9. Managing Human Resources

42. _____ describes the situation when output from (or information about the result of) an event or phenomenon in the past will influence the same event/phenomenon in the present or future. When an event is part of a chain of cause-and-effect that forms a circuit or loop, then the event is said to 'feed back' into itself.

_____ is also a synonym for:

- _____ signal; the information about the initial event that is the basis for subsequent modification of the event.
- _____ loop; the causal path that leads from the initial generation of the _____ signal to the subsequent modification of the event.

_____ is a mechanism, process or signal that is looped back to control a system within itself. Such a loop is called a _____ loop.

a. 1990 Clean Air Act
b. Feedback loop
c. Feedback
d. Positive feedback

43. In psychology research on behaviorism, _____ are scales used to report performance. _____ are normally presented vertically with scale points ranging from five to nine.

It is an appraisal method that aims to combine the benefits of narratives, critical incident incidents, and quantified ratings by anchoring a quantified scale with specific narrative examples of good or poor performance.

a. 28-hour day
b. 1990 Clean Air Act
c. 33 Strategies of War
d. Behaviorally anchored rating scales

44. A _____ is a set of categories designed to elicit information about a quantitative or a qualitative attribute. In the social sciences, common examples are the Likert scale and 1-10 _____s in which a person selects the number which is considered to reflect the perceived quality of a product.

A _____ is an instrument that requires the rater to assign the rated object that have numerals assigned to them.

a. Thurstone scale
b. Spearman-Brown prediction formula
c. Polytomous Rasch model
d. Rating scale

45. _____ is a civil designation for persons who are incorporated in a fixed or permanent way to a society or group: regular member of the working staff, permanent staff distinguished from a supernumerary.

The term '_____' and its counterpart, 'supernumerary,' originated in Spanish and Latin American academy and government; it is now also used in countries all over the world, such as France, the U.S., England, Italy, etc.

There are _____ members of surgical organizations, of universities, of gastronomical associations, etc.

a. Numerary
b. Abraham Harold Maslow
c. Affiliation
d. Adam Smith

46. _____ is unwelcome harassment of a sexual nature, or based upon the receiving party's sex or gender. In some contexts or circumstances, _____ may be illegal. It includes a range of behavior from seemingly mild transgressions and annoyances to actual sexual abuse or sexual assault.
a. Hypernorms
b. Sexual harassment
c. 28-hour day
d. 1990 Clean Air Act

47. In mainstream economic theories, the supply of labor is the number of total hours that workers wish to work at a given real wage rate. Realisticly, the _____ is a fuction of various factors within an economy. For instance, overpopulation increases the number of available workers driving down wages and can result in high unemployment.
a. Labor supply
b. 33 Strategies of War
c. 1990 Clean Air Act
d. 28-hour day

48. _____ is a term defined by the Oxford English Dictionary as an individual's 'course or progress through life '. It is usually considered to pertain to remunerative work (and sometimes also formal education.)

The etymology of the term is somewhat ironic in that it comes from the Latin word carrera, which means race .

a. Spatial mismatch
b. Career
c. Career planning
d. Nursing shortage

49. A _____ or labor union is an organization of workers who have banded together to achieve common goals in key areas and working conditions. The _____, through its leadership, bargains with the employer on behalf of union members (rank and file members) and negotiates labor contracts (Collective bargaining) with employers. This may include the negotiation of wages, work rules, complaint procedures, rules governing hiring, firing and promotion of workers, benefits, workplace safety and policies.
a. Company union
b. Working time
c. Trade union
d. Labour law

Chapter 10. Understanding Groups and Developing Effective Teams

1. _____ is a concept in ethics with several meanings. It is often used synonymously with such concepts as responsibility, answerability, enforcement, blameworthiness, liability and other terms associated with the expectation of account-giving. As an aspect of governance, it has been central to discussions related to problems in both the public and private (corporation) worlds.

    a. Usury
    b. A Stake in the Outcome
    c. Accountability
    d. A4e

2. _____ is a civil designation for persons who are incorporated in a fixed or permanent way to a society or group: regular member of the working staff, permanent staff distinguished from a supernumerary.

    The term '_____' and its counterpart, 'supernumerary,' originated in Spanish and Latin American academy and government; it is now also used in countries all over the world, such as France, the U.S., England, Italy, etc.

    There are _____ members of surgical organizations, of universities, of gastronomical associations, etc.

    a. Numerary
    b. Abraham Harold Maslow
    c. Affiliation
    d. Adam Smith

3. In the social psychology of groups, _____ is the phenomenon of people making less effort to achieve a goal when they work in a group than when they work alone. This is seen as one of the main reasons groups are sometimes less productive than the combined performance of their members working as individuals.

    - Ringelmann, Max : 1913

    Research began in 1913 with Max Ringelmann's study. He found that when he asked a group of men to pull on a rope, that they did not pull as hard, or put as much effort into the activity, as they did when they were pulling alone.

    a. Personal space
    b. Self-enhancement
    c. Machiavellianism
    d. Social loafing

4. The 'business case for _____', theorizes that in a global marketplace, a company that employs a diverse workforce (both men and women, people of many generations, people from ethnically and racially diverse backgrounds etc.) is better able to understand the demographics of the marketplace it serves and is thus better equipped to thrive in that marketplace than a company that has a more limited range of employee demographics.

Chapter 10. Understanding Groups and Developing Effective Teams 81

An additional corollary suggests that a company that supports the _____ of its workforce can also improve employee satisfaction, productivity and retention.

   a. Virtual team
   b. Diversity
   c. Trademark
   d. Kanban

5. _____ is the statistical study of all populations. It can be a very general science that can be applied to any kind of dynamic population, that is, one that changes over time or space It encompasses the study of the size, structure and distribution of populations, and spatial and/or temporal changes in them in response to birth, migration, aging and death.
   a. 28-hour day
   b. Demography
   c. 33 Strategies of War
   d. 1990 Clean Air Act

6. The _____ is the labour pool in employment. It is generally used to describe those working for a single company or industry, but can also apply to a geographic region like a city, country, state, etc. The term generally excludes the employers or management, and implies those involved in manual labour.
   a. Workforce
   b. Pink-collar worker
   c. Work-life balance
   d. Division of labour

7. _____ can be regarded as an outcome of mental processes (cognitive process) leading to the selection of a course of action among several alternatives. Every _____ process produces a final choice. The output can be an action or an opinion of choice.
   a. 33 Strategies of War
   b. Decision making
   c. 1990 Clean Air Act
   d. 28-hour day

8. _____ is a type of thought exhibited by group members who try to minimize conflict and reach consensus without critically testing, analyzing, and evaluating ideas. Individual creativity, uniqueness, and independent thinking are lost in the pursuit of group cohesiveness, as are the advantages of reasonable balance in choice and thought that might normally be obtained by making decisions as a group. During _____, members of the group avoid promoting viewpoints outside the comfort zone of consensus thinking.

Chapter 10. Understanding Groups and Developing Effective Teams

   a. Diffusion of responsibility
   b. Groupthink
   c. Self-report inventory
   d. Psychological statistics

9. _____ is decision making in groups consisting of multiple members/entities. The challenge of group decision is deciding what action a group should take. There are various systems designed to solve this problem.
   a. Collaborative Planning, Forecasting and Replenishment
   b. Genbutsu
   c. Control of Substances Hazardous to Health Regulations 2002
   d. Groups decision making

10. _____ is a group creativity technique designed to generate a large number of ideas for the solution of a problem. The method was first popularized in the late 1930s by Alex Faickney Osborn in a book called Applied Imagination. Osborn proposed that groups could double their creative output with _____.
    a. Abraham Harold Maslow
    b. Brainstorming
    c. Affiliation
    d. Adam Smith

11. In decision theory and estimation theory, the _____ of an estimator, $\hat{\theta}$, of an unknown parameter of the distribution, θ, is the expected value of the loss function

$$R(\theta, \hat{\theta}) = \mathbb{E}_\theta L(\theta, \hat{\theta}) = \int L(\theta, \hat{\theta}) \, dP_\theta.$$

Chapter 10. Understanding Groups and Developing Effective Teams

where dP_θ is a probability measure parametrized by θ.

- For a scalar parameter θ and a quadratic loss function,

$$L(\theta, \hat{\theta}) = (\theta - \hat{\theta})^2$$

the _____ function becomes the mean squared error of the estimate,

$$R(\theta, \hat{\theta}) = E_\theta(\theta - \hat{\theta})^2$$

- In density estimation, the unknown parameter is probability density itself. The loss function is typically chosen to be a norm in an appropriate function space. For example, for L^2 norm,

$$L(f, \hat{f}) = \|f - \hat{f}\|_2^2$$

the _____ function becomes the mean integrated squared error

$$R(f, \hat{f}) = E\|f - \hat{f}\|^2$$

a. Risk aversion
b. Linear model
c. Risk
d. Financial modeling

12. The _____ is a decision making method for use among groups of many sizes, who want to make their decision quickly, as by a vote, but want everyone's opinions taken into account (as opposed to traditional voting, where only the largest group is considered). The method of tallying is the difference. First, every member of the group gives their view of the solution, with a short explanation.
   a. Decision model
   b. Hierarchical Decision Process
   c. Belief decision matrix
   d. Nominal group technique

13. _____ is a family of standards for quality management systems. _____ is maintained by ISO, the International Organization for Standardization and is administered by accreditation and certification bodies. The rules are updated, the time and changes in the requirements for quality, motivate change.

a. A4e
b. A Stake in the Outcome
c. AAAI
d. ISO 9000

14. The _____ captures an expanded spectrum of values and criteria for measuring organizational success: economic, ecological and social. With the ratification of the United Nations and ICLEI _____ standard for urban and community accounting in early 2007, this became the dominant approach to public sector full cost accounting. Similar UN standards apply to natural capital and human capital measurement to assist in measurements required by _____, e.g. the ecoBudget standard for reporting ecological footprint.
    a. 1990 Clean Air Act
    b. 33 Strategies of War
    c. 28-hour day
    d. Triple bottom line

15. A _____ is a group of employees from various functional areas of the organization - research, engineering, marketing, finance. human resources, and operations, for example - who are all focused on a specific objective and are responsible to work as a team to improve coordination and innovation across divisions and resolve mutual problems.
    a. Graduate recruitment
    b. Cross-functional team
    c. Goal-setting theory
    d. Sociotechnical systems

16. A _____ -- also known as a geographically dispersed team -- is a group of individuals who work across time, space, and organizational boundaries with links strengthened by webs of communication technology. They have complementary skills and are committed to a common purpose, have interdependent performance goals, and share an approach to work for which they hold themselves mutually accountable. Geographically dispersed teams allow organizations to hire and retain the best people regardless of location.
    a. Risk management
    b. Kanban
    c. Trademark
    d. Virtual team

17. _____ is a method by which the job performance of an employee is evaluated _____ is a part of career development.

_____s are regular reviews of employee performance within organizations

Generally, the aims of a _____ are to:

- Give feedback on performance to employees.
- Identify employee training needs.
- Document criteria used to allocate organizational rewards.
- Form a basis for personnel decisions: salary increases, promotions, disciplinary actions, etc.
- Provide the opportunity for organizational diagnosis and development.
- Facilitate communication between employee and administraton
- Validate selection techniques and human resource policies to meet federal Equal Employment Opportunity requirements.

A common approach to assessing performance is to use a numerical or scalar rating system whereby managers are asked to score an individual against a number of objectives/attributes. In some companies, employees receive assessments from their manager, peers, subordinates and customers while also performing a self assessment.

a. Performance appraisal
b. Personnel management
c. Progressive discipline
d. Human resource management

18. In neuroscience, the _____ is a collection of brain structures which attempts to regulate and control behavior by inducing pleasurable effects.

A psychological reward is a process that reinforces behavior -- something that, when offered, causes a behavior to increase in intensity. Reward is an operational concept for describing the positive value an individual ascribes to an object, behavioral act or an internal physical state.

a. 33 Strategies of War
b. 28-hour day
c. 1990 Clean Air Act
d. Reward system

Chapter 11. Creating and Sustaining the Organization's Culture

1. _____ is an idea in the field of Organizational studies and management which describes the psychology, attitudes, experiences, beliefs and Values (personal and cultural values) of an organization. It has been defined as 'the specific collection of values and norms that are shared by people and groups in an organization and that control the way they interact with each other and with stakeholders outside the organization.'

This definition continues to explain organizational values also known as 'beliefs and ideas about what kinds of goals members of an organization should pursue and ideas about the appropriate kinds or standards of behavior organizational members should use to achieve these goals. From organizational values develop organizational norms, guidelines or expectations that prescribe appropriate kinds of behavior by employees in particular situations and control the behavior of organizational members towards one another.'

_____ is not the same as corporate culture.

 a. Union shop
 b. Organizational effectiveness
 c. Organizational development
 d. Organizational culture

2. _____ is a civil designation for persons who are incorporated in a fixed or permanent way to a society or group: regular member of the working staff, permanent staff distinguished from a supernumerary.

The term '_____' and its counterpart, 'supernumerary,' originated in Spanish and Latin American academy and government; it is now also used in countries all over the world, such as France, the U.S., England, Italy, etc.

There are _____ members of surgical organizations, of universities, of gastronomical associations, etc.

 a. Adam Smith
 b. Numerary
 c. Abraham Harold Maslow
 d. Affiliation

3. In sociology, anthropology and cultural studies, a _____ is a group of people with a culture (whether distinct or hidden) which differentiates them from the larger culture to which they belong. If a particular _____ is characterized by a systematic opposition to the dominant culture, it may be described as a counterculture.

As early as 1950, David Riesman distinguished between a majority, 'which passively accepted commercially provided styles and meanings, and a '_____' which actively sought a minority style ...

Chapter 11. Creating and Sustaining the Organization`s Culture

a. 33 Strategies of War
b. 28-hour day
c. 1990 Clean Air Act
d. Subculture

4. The _____ assessment is a psychometric questionnaire designed to measure psychological preferences in how people perceive the world and make decisions.[1] These preferences were extrapolated from the typological theories originated by Carl Gustav Jung, as published in his 1921 book Psychological Types . The original developers of the personality inventory were Katharine Cook Briggs and her daughter, Isabel Briggs Myers. They began creating the indicator during World War II, believing that a knowledge of personality preferences would help women who were entering the industrial workforce for the first time identify the sort of war-time jobs where they would be 'most comfortable and effective'.[xiii] The initial questionnaire grew into the _____, which was first published in 1962.
  a. 1990 Clean Air Act
  b. Myers-Briggs Type Indicator
  c. 33 Strategies of War
  d. 28-hour day

5. The 'business case for _____', theorizes that in a global marketplace, a company that employs a diverse workforce (both men and women, people of many generations, people from ethnically and racially diverse backgrounds etc.) is better able to understand the demographics of the marketplace it serves and is thus better equipped to thrive in that marketplace than a company that has a more limited range of employee demographics.

An additional corollary suggests that a company that supports the _____ of its workforce can also improve employee satisfaction, productivity and retention.

  a. Kanban
  b. Trademark
  c. Diversity
  d. Virtual team

6. The _____ is the labour pool in employment. It is generally used to describe those working for a single company or industry, but can also apply to a geographic region like a city, country, state, etc. The term generally excludes the employers or management, and implies those involved in manual labour.
  a. Workforce
  b. Division of labour
  c. Pink-collar worker
  d. Work-life balance

Chapter 12. Understanding the Basics of Human Behavior

1. The _____ assessment is a psychometric questionnaire designed to measure psychological preferences in how people perceive the world and make decisions.[1] These preferences were extrapolated from the typological theories originated by Carl Gustav Jung, as published in his 1921 book Psychological Types . The original developers of the personality inventory were Katharine Cook Briggs and her daughter, Isabel Briggs Myers. They began creating the indicator during World War II, believing that a knowledge of personality preferences would help women who were entering the industrial workforce for the first time identify the sort of war-time jobs where they would be 'most comfortable and effective'.[xiii] The initial questionnaire grew into the _____, which was first published in 1962.

   a. Myers-Briggs Type Indicator
   b. 28-hour day
   c. 33 Strategies of War
   d. 1990 Clean Air Act

2. _____ is a term in psychology which refers to a person's belief about what causes the good or bad results in his or her life, either in general or in a specific area such as health or academics. Understanding of the concept was developed by Julian B. Rotter in 1954, and has since become an important aspect of personality studies.

   _____ refers to the extent to which individuals believe that they can control events that affect them.

   a. Locus of control
   b. Social loafing
   c. Self-enhancement
   d. Machiavellianism

3. _____ is a way of expressing knowledge or belief that an event will occur or has occurred. In mathematics the concept has been given an exact meaning in _____ theory, that is used extensively in such areas of study as mathematics, statistics, finance, gambling, science, and philosophy to draw conclusions about the likelihood of potential events and the underlying mechanics of complex systems.

   The word _____ does not have a consistent direct definition.

   a. Standard deviation
   b. Statistics
   c. Time series analysis
   d. Probability

4. _____ is one of the managerial functions like planning, organizing, staffing and directing. It is an important function because it helps to check the errors and to take the corrective action so that deviation from standards are minimized and stated goals of the organization are achieved in desired manner.According to modern concepts, _____ is a foreseeing action whereas earlier concept of _____ was used only when errors were detected. _____ in management means setting standards, measuring actual performance and taking corrective action.

a. Control
b. Schedule of reinforcement
c. Turnover
d. Decision tree pruning

5. The _____ captures an expanded spectrum of values and criteria for measuring organizational success: economic, ecological and social. With the ratification of the United Nations and ICLEI _____ standard for urban and community accounting in early 2007, this became the dominant approach to public sector full cost accounting. Similar UN standards apply to natural capital and human capital measurement to assist in measurements required by _____, e.g. the ecoBudget standard for reporting ecological footprint.

a. 1990 Clean Air Act
b. 28-hour day
c. 33 Strategies of War
d. Triple bottom line

6. _____ is, according to the OED, 'the employment of cunning and duplicity in statecraft or in general conduct', deriving from the Italian Renaissance diplomat and writer Niccolò Machiavelli, who wrote Il Principe and other works. Machiavellian and variants became very popular in the late 16th century in English, though '_____' itself is first cited by the OED from 1626. The word has a similar use in modern psychology.

a. Persuasion
b. Self-enhancement
c. Personal space
d. Machiavellianism

7. In psychology, _____ reflects a person's overall evaluation or appraisal of his or her own worth.

_____ encompasses beliefs (for example, 'I am competent/incompetent') and emotions (for example, triumph/despair, pride/shame.) Behavior may reflect _____

a. 1990 Clean Air Act
b. 33 Strategies of War
c. Self-esteem
d. 28-hour day

8. In statistics, _____ is:

   - the arithmetic _____
   - the expected value of a random variable, which is also called the population _____.

It is sometimes stated that the '_____' _____s average. This is incorrect if '_____' is taken in the specific sense of 'arithmetic _____' as there are different types of averages: the _____, median, and mode. Other simple statistical analyses use measures of spread, such as range, interquartile range, or standard deviation. For a real-valued random variable X, the _____ is the expectation of X. Note that not every probability distribution has a defined _____; see the Cauchy distribution for an example.

a. Mean
b. Correlation
c. Control chart
d. Statistical inference

9. In decision theory and estimation theory, the _____ of an estimator, $\hat{\theta}$, of an unknown parameter of the distribution, θ, is the expected value of the loss function

$$R(\theta, \hat{\theta}) = \mathbb{E}_\theta L(\theta, \hat{\theta}) = \int L(\theta, \hat{\theta})\, dP_\theta.$$

where dP_θ is a probability measure parametrized by θ.

- For a scalar parameter θ and a quadratic loss function,

$$L(\theta, \hat{\theta}) = (\theta - \hat{\theta})^2$$

the _____ function becomes the mean squared error of the estimate,

$$R(\theta, \hat{\theta}) = E_\theta (\theta - \hat{\theta})^2$$

- In density estimation, the unknown parameter is probability density itself. The loss function is typically chosen to be a norm in an appropriate function space. For example, for L^2 norm,

$$L(f, \hat{f}) = \|f - \hat{f}\|_2^2$$

the _____ function becomes the mean integrated squared error

$$R(f, \hat{f}) = E\|f - \hat{f}\|^2$$

a. Risk aversion
b. Linear model
c. Risk
d. Financial modeling

10. The _____ is a personality type theory that describes a pattern of behaviors that were once considered to be a risk factor for coronary heart disease. Since its inception in the 1950s, the theory has been widely popularized and also widely criticised for its scientific shortcomings.

Type A individuals can be described as impatient, excessively time-conscious, insecure about their status, highly competitive, over-ambitious, business-like, hostile, aggressive, incapable of relaxation in taking the smallest issues too seriously; and are somewhat disliked for the way that they're always rushing and demanding other people to serve to their standards of satisfaction.

a. 33 Strategies of War
b. 1990 Clean Air Act
c. 28-hour day
d. Type A and Type B personality theory

11. In a human resources context, _____ or labor _____ is the rate at which an employer gains and loses employees. Simple ways to describe it are 'how long employees tend to stay' or 'the rate of traffic through the revolving door.' _____ is measured for individual companies and for their industry as a whole. If an employer is said to have a high _____ relative to its competitors, it means that employees of that company have a shorter average tenure than those of other companies in the same industry.
   a. Turnover
   b. Continuous
   c. Ten year occupational employment projection
   d. Career portfolios

12. _____ is a social psychology theory developed by Fritz Heider, Harold Kelley, Edward E. Jones, and Lee Ross.

The theory is concerned with the ways in which people explain (or attribute) the behavior of others or themselves (self-attribution) with something else. It explores how individuals 'attribute' causes to events and how this cognitive perception effects their usefulness in an organization.

   a. Attribution theory
   b. AAAI
   c. A Stake in the Outcome
   d. A4e

13. In attribution theory, the _____ is a theory describing cognitive tendency to predominantly over-value dispositional explanations for the observed behaviors of others, thus under-valuing or acknowledging the potentiality of situational attributions or situational explanations for the behavioral motives of others. In other words, people predominantly presume that the actions of others are indicative of the 'kind' of person they are, rather than the kind of situations that compels their behavior. However, the over attribution effect generally does not account for our own ability to self-justify our behaviors; we tend to prefer interpreting our own actions in terms of the situational variables accessible to our awareness.
   a. Pygmalion effect
   b. Confirmation bias
   c. Halo effect
   d. Fundamental attribution error

Chapter 12. Understanding the Basics of Human Behavior

14. A _____ occurs when people attribute their successes to internal or personal factors but attribute their failures to situational factors beyond their control. The _____ can be seen in the common human tendency to take credit for success but to deny responsibility for failure. It may also manifest itself as a tendency for people to evaluate ambiguous information in a way that is beneficial to their interests.
   a. Pygmalion effect
   b. Fundamental attribution error
   c. Self-serving bias
   d. Halo effect

15. The _____ refers to a cognitive bias whereby the perception of a particular trait is influenced by the perception of the former traits in a sequence of interpretations.

Edward L. Thorndike was the first to support the _____ with empirical research. In a psychology study published in 1920, Thorndike asked commanding officers to rate their soldiers; Thorndike found high cross-correlation between all positive and all negative traits.

   a. Cognitive biases
   b. Sunk costs
   c. Distinction bias
   d. Halo effect

16. The _____ refers to situations in which students perform better than other students simply because they are expected to do so. The effect is named after George Bernard Shaw's play Pygmalion, in which a professor makes a bet that he can teach a poor flower girl to speak and act like an upper-class lady, and is successful.

The _____ requires a student to internalize the expectations of their superiors.

   a. Distinction bias
   b. Confirmation bias
   c. Halo effect
   d. Pygmalion effect

17. A _____ is a prediction that directly or indirectly causes itself to become true, by the very terms of the prophecy itself, due to positive feedback between belief and behavior. Although examples of such prophecies can be found in literature as far back as ancient Greece and ancient India, it is 20th-century sociologist Robert K. Merton who is credited with coining the expression '_____' and formalizing its structure and consequences. In his book Social Theory and Social Structure, Merton gives as a feature of the _____:

In other words, a prophecy declared as truth when it is actually false may sufficiently influence people, either through fear or logical confusion, so that their reactions ultimately fulfill the once-false prophecy.

Chapter 12. Understanding the Basics of Human Behavior

   a. 33 Strategies of War
   b. 28-hour day
   c. 1990 Clean Air Act
   d. Self-fulfilling prophecy

18. _____ describes how content an individual is with his or her job.

The happier people are within their job, the more satisfied they are said to be. _____ is not the same as motivation, although it is clearly linked.

   a. Goal-setting theory
   b. Job satisfaction
   c. Human relations
   d. Job analysis

19. _____ is an uncomfortable feeling caused by holding two contradictory ideas simultaneously. The 'ideas' or 'cognitions' in question may include attitudes and beliefs, and also the awareness of one's behavior. The theory of _____ proposes that people have a motivational drive to reduce dissonance by changing their attitudes, beliefs, and behaviors, or by justifying or rationalizing their attitudes, beliefs, and behaviors.
   a. Cognitive bias
   b. Trait theory
   c. Quantitative psychology
   d. Cognitive dissonance

20. _____ refers to metrics and measures of output from production processes, per unit of input. Labor _____, for example, is typically measured as a ratio of output per labor-hour, an input. _____ may be conceived of as a metrics of the technical or engineering efficiency of production.
   a. Value engineering
   b. Productivity
   c. Master production schedule
   d. Remanufacturing

21. _____ consists of the mental process of thinking involved with the process of judging the merits of multiple options and selecting one of them for action. Some simple examples include deciding whether to get up in the morning or go back to sleep, or selecting a given route for a journey. More complex examples (often decisions that affect what a person thinks or their core beliefs) include choosing a lifestyle, religious affiliation, or political position.

Chapter 12. Understanding the Basics of Human Behavior

a. Trade study
b. Groups decision making
c. Championship mobilization
d. Choice

22. _____ is the use of consequences to modify the occurrence and form of behavior. _____ is distinguished from classical conditioning (also called respondent conditioning, or Pavlovian conditioning) in that _____ deals with the modification of 'voluntary behavior' or operant behavior. Operant behavior 'operates' on the environment and is maintained by its consequences, while classical conditioning deals with the conditioning of respondent behaviors which are elicited by antecedent conditions.
    a. Operant conditioning
    b. Occupational Safety and Health Administration
    c. Unemployment insurance
    d. Outsourcing

23. _____ refers to training in different ways to improve overall performance. It takes advantage of the particular effectiveness of each training method, while at the same time attempting to neglect the shortcomings of that method by combining it with other methods that address its weaknesses.

Cross training is employee-employer field means, training employees to do one another's work.

    a. 28-hour day
    b. 33 Strategies of War
    c. 1990 Clean Air Act
    d. Cross-training

24. In operant conditioning, _____ occurs when an event following a response causes an increase in the probability of that response occurring in the future. Response strength can be assessed by measures such as the frequency with which the response is made (for example, a pigeon may peck a key more times in the session), or the speed with which it is made (for example, a rat may run a maze faster.) The environment change contingent upon the response is called a reinforcer.
    a. Historiometry
    b. Diminishing Manufacturing Sources and Material Shortages
    c. Reinforcement
    d. Meetings, Incentives, Conferences, and Exhibitions

Chapter 12. Understanding the Basics of Human Behavior

25. In probability theory, a probability distribution is called _____ if its cumulative distribution function is _____. This is equivalent to saying that for random variables X with the distribution in question, Pr[X = a] = 0 for all real numbers a, i.e.: the probability that X attains the value a is zero, for any number a. If the distribution of X is _____ then X is called a _____ random variable.
   a. Continuous
   b. Pay Band
   c. Decision tree pruning
   d. Connectionist expert systems

26. When an animal's surroundings are controlled, its behavior patterns after reinforcement become predictable, even for very complex behavior patterns. A schedule of reinforcement is the protocol for determining when responses or behaviors will be reinforced, ranging from _____, in which every response is reinforced, and extinction, in which no response is reinforced. Between these extremes is intermittent or partial reinforcement where only some responses are reinforced.
   a. Clinical decision support systems
   b. Pension System
   c. Recognition-primed decision
   d. Continuous reinforcement

Chapter 13. Work Motivation and Rewards

1. Clayton Paul Alderfer is an American psychologist who further expanded Maslow's hierarchy of needs by categorizing the hierarchy into his _____ Alderfer categorized the lower order needs (Physiological and Safety) into the Existence category. He fit Maslow's interpersonal love and esteem needs into the relatedness category. The growth category contained the Self Actualization and self esteem needs.

   Alderfer also proposed a regression theory to go along with the _____. He said that when needs in a higher category are not met then individuals redouble the efforts invested in a lower category need.

   a. Abraham Harold Maslow
   b. ERG theory
   c. Adam Smith
   d. Alvin Neill Jackson

2. In neuroscience, the _____ is a collection of brain structures which attempts to regulate and control behavior by inducing pleasurable effects.

   A psychological reward is a process that reinforces behavior -- something that, when offered, causes a behavior to increase in intensity. Reward is an operational concept for describing the positive value an individual ascribes to an object, behavioral act or an internal physical state.

   a. Reward system
   b. 33 Strategies of War
   c. 1990 Clean Air Act
   d. 28-hour day

3. _____ can be regarded as an outcome of mental processes (cognitive process) leading to the selection of a course of action among several alternatives. Every _____ process produces a final choice. The output can be an action or an opinion of choice.
   a. 33 Strategies of War
   b. 28-hour day
   c. 1990 Clean Air Act
   d. Decision making

4. Maslow's _____ is a theory in psychology, proposed by Abraham Maslow in his 1943 paper A Theory of Human Motivation, which he subsequently extended to include his observations of humans' innate curiosity.

   Maslow's _____ is predetermined in order of importance. It is often depicted as a pyramid consisting of five levels: the lowest level is associated with physiological needs, while the uppermost level is associated with self-actualization needs, particularly those related to identity and purpose. Deficiency needs must be met first. Once these are met, seeking to satisfy growth needs drives personal growth. The higher needs in this hierarchy only come into focus when the lower needs in the pyramid are met.

Chapter 13. Work Motivation and Rewards

a. 28-hour day
b. 1990 Clean Air Act
c. 33 Strategies of War
d. Hierarchy of needs

5. In game theory, an _____ is a set of moves or strategies taken by the players, or their payoffs resulting from the actions or strategies taken by all players. The two are complementary in that given knowledge of the set of strategies of all players, the final state of the game is known, as are any relevant payoffs. In a game where chance or a random event is involved, the _____ is not known from only the set of strategies, but is only realized when the random event(s) are realized.
   a. A4e
   b. A Stake in the Outcome
   c. Outcome
   d. AAAI

6. _____ is a term that has been used in various psychology theories, often in slightly different ways (e.g., Goldstein, Maslow, Rogers.) The term was originally introduced by the organismic theorist Kurt Goldstein for the motive to realise all of one's potentialities. In his view, it is the master motive--indeed, the only real motive a person has, all others being merely manifestations of it.
   a. 1990 Clean Air Act
   b. 28-hour day
   c. 33 Strategies of War
   d. Self-actualization

7. _____ is an organization's process of defining its strategy and making decisions on allocating its resources to pursue this strategy, including its capital and people. Various business analysis techniques can be used in _____, including SWOT analysis (Strengths, Weaknesses, Opportunities, and Threats) and PEST analysis (Political, Economic, Social, and Technological analysis) or STEER analysis involving Socio-cultural, Technological, Economic, Ecological, and Regulatory factors and EPISTEL (Environment, Political, Informatic, Social, Technological, Economic and Legal)

_____ is the formal consideration of an organization's future course. All _____ deals with at least one of three key questions:

   1. 'What do we do?'
   2. 'For whom do we do it?'
   3. 'How do we excel?'

In business _____, the third question is better phrased 'How can we beat or avoid competition?'. (Bradford and Duncan, page 1.)

Chapter 13. Work Motivation and Rewards

a. 33 Strategies of War
b. 28-hour day
c. 1990 Clean Air Act
d. Strategic planning

8. In law, _____ is the term to describe a partnership between two or more parties.

In England a number of statutes on the subject have been passed, the chief being the Bastardy Act of 1845, and the Bastardy Laws Amendment Acts of 1872 and 1873. The mother of a bastard may summon the putative father to petty sessions within twelve months of the birth (or at any later time if he is proved to have contributed to the child's support within twelve months after the birth), and the justices, as after hearing evidence on both sides, may, if the mother's evidence be corroborated in some material particular, adjudge the man to be the putative father of the child, and order him to pay a sum not exceeding five shillings a week for its maintenance, together with a sum for expenses incidental to the birth, or the funeral expenses, if it has died before the date of order, and the costs of the proceedings.

a. Affiliation
b. Adam Smith
c. Affirmative action
d. Abraham Harold Maslow

9. _____ and Theory Y are theories of human motivation created and developed by Douglas McGregor at the MIT Sloan School of Management in the 1960s that have been used in human resource management, organizational behavior, organizational communication and organizational development. They describe two very different attitudes toward workforce motivation. McGregor felt that companies followed either one or the other approach.

In _____, which many managers practice, management assumes employees are inherently lazy and will avoid work if they can. They inherently dislike work. Because of this, workers need to be closely supervised and comprehensive systems of controls developed.

a. Theory X
b. Job enrichment
c. Cash cow
d. Management team

10. Theory X and _____ are theories of human motivation created and developed by Douglas McGregor at the MIT Sloan School of Management in the 1960s that have been used in human resource management, organizational behavior, organizational communication and organizational development. They describe two very different attitudes toward workforce motivation. McGregor felt that companies followed either one or the other approach.

In _____, management assumes employees may be ambitious and self-motivated and exercise self-control. It is believed that employees enjoy their mental and physical work duties.

a. Contingency theory
b. Theory Y
c. Business Workflow Analysis
d. Design leadership

11. _____ describes how content an individual is with his or her job.

The happier people are within their job, the more satisfied they are said to be. _____ is not the same as motivation, although it is clearly linked.

a. Job satisfaction
b. Job analysis
c. Human relations
d. Goal-setting theory

12. _____ has become one of the most popular theories in organizational psychology.

Goal setting has been a formula used for acheivement since the early 1800s. The form and pattern has cahanged drastically over the years and there is still much debate as to what is the most efective pattern to follow.

a. Corporate Culture
b. Human relations
c. Job satisfaction
d. Goal-setting theory

13. _____ describes the situation when output from (or information about the result of) an event or phenomenon in the past will influence the same event/phenomenon in the present or future. When an event is part of a chain of cause-and-effect that forms a circuit or loop, then the event is said to 'feed back' into itself.

Chapter 13. Work Motivation and Rewards

_____ is also a synonym for:

- _____ signal; the information about the initial event that is the basis for subsequent modification of the event.
- _____ loop; the causal path that leads from the initial generation of the _____ signal to the subsequent modification of the event.

_____ is a mechanism, process or signal that is looped back to control a system within itself. Such a loop is called a _____ loop.

a. Feedback
b. Positive feedback
c. 1990 Clean Air Act
d. Feedback loop

14. In operant conditioning, _____ occurs when an event following a response causes an increase in the probability of that response occurring in the future. Response strength can be assessed by measures such as the frequency with which the response is made (for example, a pigeon may peck a key more times in the session), or the speed with which it is made (for example, a rat may run a maze faster.) The environment change contingent upon the response is called a reinforcer.
a. Reinforcement
b. Meetings, Incentives, Conferences, and Exhibitions
c. Historiometry
d. Diminishing Manufacturing Sources and Material Shortages

15. _____ is the belief that one is capable of performing in a certain manner to attain certain goals. It is a belief that one has the capabilities to execute the courses of actions required to manage prospective situations. Unlike efficacy, which is the power to produce an effect (in essence, competence), _____ is the belief (whether or not accurate) that one has the power to produce that effect.
a. Self-efficacy
b. 28-hour day
c. 1990 Clean Air Act
d. 33 Strategies of War

16. _____ attempts to explain relational satisfaction in terms of perceptions of fair/unfair distributions of resources within interpersonal relationships. _____ is considered as one of the justice theories, It was first developed in 1962 by John Stacey Adams, a workplace and behavioral psychologist, who asserted that employees seek to maintain equity between the inputs that they bring to a job and the outcomes that they receive from it against the perceived inputs and outcomes of others (Adams, 1965.) The belief is that people value fair treatment which causes them to be motivated to keep the fairness maintained within the relationships of their co-workers and the organization.

Chapter 13. Work Motivation and Rewards

   a. A Stake in the Outcome
   b. AAAI
   c. Equity theory
   d. A4e

17. _____ is about the mental processes regarding choice, or choosing. It explains the processes that an individual undergoes to make choices. In organizational behavior study, _____ is a motivation theory first proposed by Victor Vroom of the Yale School of Management.
   a. A Stake in the Outcome
   b. A4e
   c. AAAI
   d. Expectancy theory

18. An _____ is a natural person, business, or corporation which provides goods or services to another entity under terms specified in a contract or within a verbal agreement. Unlike an employee, an _____ does not work regularly for an employer but works as and when required, during which time she or he may be subject to the Law of Agency. _____s are usually paid on a freelance basis.
   a. Occupational Safety and Health Act
   b. Independent contractor
   c. Employment protection legislation
   d. Equal Pay Act of 1963

19. A _____ is a professional who provides advice in a particular area of expertise such as management, accountancy, the environment, entertainment, technology, law , human resources, marketing, medicine, finance, economics, public affairs, communication, engineering, sound system design, graphic design, or waste management.

A _____ is usually an expert or a professional in a specific field and has a wide knowledge of the subject matter. A _____ usually works for a consultancy firm or is self-employed, and engages with multiple and changing clients.

   a. 1990 Clean Air Act
   b. 33 Strategies of War
   c. 28-hour day
   d. Consultant

20. _____ is an advertisement in which a particular product specifically mentions a competitor by name for the express purpose of showing why the competitor is inferior to the product naming it.

This should not be confused with parody advertisements, where a fictional product is being advertised for the purpose of poking fun at the particular advertisement, nor should it be confused with the use of a coined brand name for the purpose of comparing the product without actually naming an actual competitor. ('Wikipedia tastes better and is less filling than the Encyclopedia Galactica.')

In the 1980s, during what has been referred to as the cola wars, soft-drink manufacturer Pepsi ran a series of advertisements where people, caught on hidden camera, in a blind taste test, chose Pepsi over rival Coca-Cola.

a. 28-hour day
b. 1990 Clean Air Act
c. 33 Strategies of War
d. Comparative advertising

21. _____ is an arrangement which involves workers making decisions, sharing responsibility and authority in the workplace. In company law, the term generally used is co-determination, following the German word Mitbestimmung. In Germany half of the supervisory board of directors is elected by the shareholders, and the other half by the workers.
a. A4e
b. Industrial democracy
c. AAAI
d. A Stake in the Outcome

22. _____ is a management technique pioneered by Michael Phillips in San Francisco in the late '60's and early '70s. The concept's most visible success was by Jack Stack and his team at SRC Holdings and popularized in 1995 by John Case. The technique is to give employees all relevant financial information about the company so they can make better decisions as workers.
a. A Stake in the Outcome
b. AAAI
c. Open-book management
d. A4e

23. A _____ is a form of periodic payment from an employer to an employee, which may be specified in an employment contract. It is contrasted with piece wages, where each job, hour or other unit is paid separately, rather than on a periodic basis.

From the point of a view of running a business, _____ can also be viewed as the cost of acquiring human resources for running operations, and is then termed personnel expense or _____ expense.

a. Human resources
b. Salary
c. Training and development
d. Human resource management

24. The 'business case for _____', theorizes that in a global marketplace, a company that employs a diverse workforce (both men and women, people of many generations, people from ethnically and racially diverse backgrounds etc.) is better able to understand the demographics of the marketplace it serves and is thus better equipped to thrive in that marketplace than a company that has a more limited range of employee demographics.

An additional corollary suggests that a company that supports the _____ of its workforce can also improve employee satisfaction, productivity and retention.

a. Kanban
b. Trademark
c. Virtual team
d. Diversity

25. The _____ is the labour pool in employment. It is generally used to describe those working for a single company or industry, but can also apply to a geographic region like a city, country, state, etc. The term generally excludes the employers or management, and implies those involved in manual labour.
a. Work-life balance
b. Division of labour
c. Pink-collar worker
d. Workforce

Chapter 14. Basic Issues in Leadership

1. _____ has been described as the 'process of social influence in which one person can enlist the aid and support of others in the accomplishment of a common task'. A definition more inclusive of followers comes from Alan Keith of Genentech who said '_____ is ultimately about creating a way for people to contribute to making something extraordinary happen.'

_____ is one of the most salient aspects of the organizational context. However, defining _____ has been challenging.

   a. 1990 Clean Air Act
   b. Situational leadership
   c. 28-hour day
   d. Leadership

2. The _____ captures an expanded spectrum of values and criteria for measuring organizational success: economic, ecological and social. With the ratification of the United Nations and ICLEI _____ standard for urban and community accounting in early 2007, this became the dominant approach to public sector full cost accounting. Similar UN standards apply to natural capital and human capital measurement to assist in measurements required by _____, e.g. the ecoBudget standard for reporting ecological footprint.
   a. Triple bottom line
   b. 1990 Clean Air Act
   c. 33 Strategies of War
   d. 28-hour day

3. The _____ system was developed by AMD in the mid-1990s as a method of comparing their x86 processors to those of rival Intel.

The first use of the _____ system was in 1996, when AMD used it to assert that their AMD 5x86 processor was as fast as a Pentium running at 75 MHz. The designation 'P75' was added to the chip to denote this.

   a. 33 Strategies of War
   b. 1990 Clean Air Act
   c. 28-hour day
   d. Performance rating

4. In a human resources context, _____ or labor _____ is the rate at which an employer gains and loses employees. Simple ways to describe it are 'how long employees tend to stay' or 'the rate of traffic through the revolving door.' _____ is measured for individual companies and for their industry as a whole. If an employer is said to have a high _____ relative to its competitors, it means that employees of that company have a shorter average tenure than those of other companies in the same industry.

a. Career portfolios
b. Continuous
c. Ten year occupational employment projection
d. Turnover

5. _____ can be regarded as an outcome of mental processes (cognitive process) leading to the selection of a course of action among several alternatives. Every _____ process produces a final choice. The output can be an action or an opinion of choice.
   a. 28-hour day
   b. 1990 Clean Air Act
   c. 33 Strategies of War
   d. Decision making

6. _____ is one of the managerial functions like planning, organizing, staffing and directing. It is an important function because it helps to check the errors and to take the corrective action so that deviation from standards are minimized and stated goals of the organization are achieved in desired manner. According to modern concepts, _____ is a foreseeing action whereas earlier concept of _____ was used only when errors were detected. _____ in management means setting standards, measuring actual performance and taking corrective action.
   a. Schedule of reinforcement
   b. Decision tree pruning
   c. Turnover
   d. Control

7. The _____ is a leadership theory in the field of organizational studies developed by Robert House in 1971 and revised in 1996. The theory that a leader's behavior is contingent to the satisfaction, motivation and performance of subordinates. The revised version also argues that the leader engage in behaviors that complement subordinate's abilities and compensate for deficiencies.
   a. Human relations
   b. Corporate Culture
   c. Sociotechnical systems
   d. Path-goal theory

8. _____ is an organization's process of defining its strategy and making decisions on allocating its resources to pursue this strategy, including its capital and people. Various business analysis techniques can be used in _____, including SWOT analysis (Strengths, Weaknesses, Opportunities, and Threats) and PEST analysis (Political, Economic, Social, and Technological analysis) or STEER analysis involving Socio-cultural, Technological, Economic, Ecological, and Regulatory factors and EPISTEL (Environment, Political, Informatic, Social, Technological, Economic and Legal)

Chapter 14. Basic Issues in Leadership   107

_____ is the formal consideration of an organization's future course. All _____ deals with at least one of three key questions:

1. 'What do we do?'
2. 'For whom do we do it?'
3. 'How do we excel?'

In business _____, the third question is better phrased 'How can we beat or avoid competition?'. (Bradford and Duncan, page 1.)

a. 33 Strategies of War
b. 28-hour day
c. Strategic planning
d. 1990 Clean Air Act

9. _____ is an idea in the field of Organizational studies and management which describes the psychology, attitudes, experiences, beliefs and Values (personal and cultural values) of an organization. It has been defined as 'the specific collection of values and norms that are shared by people and groups in an organization and that control the way they interact with each other and with stakeholders outside the organization.'

This definition continues to explain organizational values also known as 'beliefs and ideas about what kinds of goals members of an organization should pursue and ideas about the appropriate kinds or standards of behavior organizational members should use to achieve these goals. From organizational values develop organizational norms, guidelines or expectations that prescribe appropriate kinds of behavior by employees in particular situations and control the behavior of organizational members towards one another.'

_____ is not the same as corporate culture.

a. Organizational development
b. Organizational effectiveness
c. Organizational culture
d. Union shop

10. _____ is a civil designation for persons who are incorporated in a fixed or permanent way to a society or group: regular member of the working staff, permanent staff distinguished from a supernumerary.

The term '_____' and its counterpart, 'supernumerary,' originated in Spanish and Latin American academy and government; it is now also used in countries all over the world, such as France, the U.S., England, Italy, etc.

There are _____ members of surgical organizations, of universities, of gastronomical associations, etc.

a. Abraham Harold Maslow
b. Affiliation
c. Adam Smith
d. Numerary

Chapter 15. Contemporary Issues in Leadership

1. _____ has been described as the 'process of social influence in which one person can enlist the aid and support of others in the accomplishment of a common task' . A definition more inclusive of followers comes from Alan Keith of Genentech who said '_____ is ultimately about creating a way for people to contribute to making something extraordinary happen.'

_____ is one of the most salient aspects of the organizational context. However, defining _____ has been challenging.

a. 1990 Clean Air Act
b. Leadership
c. 28-hour day
d. Situational leadership

2. The _____ captures an expanded spectrum of values and criteria for measuring organizational success: economic, ecological and social. With the ratification of the United Nations and ICLEI _____ standard for urban and community accounting in early 2007, this became the dominant approach to public sector full cost accounting. Similar UN standards apply to natural capital and human capital measurement to assist in measurements required by _____, e.g. the ecoBudget standard for reporting ecological footprint.

a. 28-hour day
b. 1990 Clean Air Act
c. 33 Strategies of War
d. Triple bottom line

3. _____ is an organization's process of defining its strategy and making decisions on allocating its resources to pursue this strategy, including its capital and people. Various business analysis techniques can be used in _____, including SWOT analysis (Strengths, Weaknesses, Opportunities, and Threats) and PEST analysis (Political, Economic, Social, and Technological analysis) or STEER analysis involving Socio-cultural, Technological, Economic, Ecological, and Regulatory factors and EPISTEL (Environment, Political, Informatic, Social, Technological, Economic and Legal)

_____ is the formal consideration of an organization's future course. All _____ deals with at least one of three key questions:

1. 'What do we do?'
2. 'For whom do we do it?'
3. 'How do we excel?'

In business _____, the third question is better phrased 'How can we beat or avoid competition?'. (Bradford and Duncan, page 1.)

a. 33 Strategies of War
b. Strategic planning
c. 1990 Clean Air Act
d. 28-hour day

4. The sociologist Max Weber defined _____ as 'resting on devotion to the exceptional sanctity, heroism or exemplary character of an individual person, and of the normative patterns or order revealed or ordained by him.' _____ is one of three forms of authority laid out in Weber's tripartite classification of authority, the other two being traditional authority and rational-legal authority. The concept has acquired wide usage among sociologists.

In his writings about _____, Weber applies the term charisma to 'a certain quality of an individual personality, by virtue of which he is set apart from ordinary men and treated as endowed with supernatural, superhuman, or at least specifically exceptional powers or qualities.

a. 28-hour day
b. 1990 Clean Air Act
c. Rational-legal authority
d. Charismatic authority

5. _____ is a civil designation for persons who are incorporated in a fixed or permanent way to a society or group: regular member of the working staff, permanent staff distinguished from a supernumerary.

The term '_____' and its counterpart, 'supernumerary,' originated in Spanish and Latin American academy and government; it is now also used in countries all over the world, such as France, the U.S., England, Italy, etc.

There are _____ members of surgical organizations, of universities, of gastronomical associations, etc.

a. Affiliation
b. Adam Smith
c. Abraham Harold Maslow
d. Numerary

6. There are two types of _____ relationships: formal and informal. Informal relationships develop on their own between partners. Formal _____, on the other hand, refers to assigned relationships, often associated with organizational _____ programs designed to promote employee development or to assist at-risk children and youth.

a. Human resource management system
b. Fix it twice
c. Real Property Administrator
d. Mentoring

7. _____ is one of the managerial functions like planning, organizing, staffing and directing. It is an important function because it helps to check the errors and to take the corrective action so that deviation from standards are minimized and stated goals of the organization are achieved in desired manner.According to modern concepts, _____ is a foreseeing action whereas earlier concept of _____ was used only when errors were detected. _____ in management means setting standards, measuring actual performance and taking corrective action.
   a. Decision tree pruning
   b. Schedule of reinforcement
   c. Turnover
   d. Control

8. The 'business case for _____', theorizes that in a global marketplace, a company that employs a diverse workforce (both men and women, people of many generations, people from ethnically and racially diverse backgrounds etc.) is better able to understand the demographics of the marketplace it serves and is thus better equipped to thrive in that marketplace than a company that has a more limited range of employee demographics.

An additional corollary suggests that a company that supports the _____ of its workforce can also improve employee satisfaction, productivity and retention.

   a. Virtual team
   b. Kanban
   c. Trademark
   d. Diversity

9. The _____ is the labour pool in employment. It is generally used to describe those working for a single company or industry, but can also apply to a geographic region like a city, country, state, etc. The term generally excludes the employers or management, and implies those involved in manual labour.
   a. Pink-collar worker
   b. Work-life balance
   c. Workforce
   d. Division of labour

1. _____ is a social psychology theory developed by Fritz Heider, Harold Kelley, Edward E. Jones, and Lee Ross.

The theory is concerned with the ways in which people explain (or attribute) the behavior of others or themselves (self-attribution) with something else. It explores how individuals 'attribute' causes to events and how this cognitive perception effects their usefulness in an organization.

    a. A Stake in the Outcome
    b. A4e
    c. Attribution theory
    d. AAAI

2. A _____ represents the mutual beliefs, perceptions, and informal obligations between an employer and an employee. It sets the dynamics for the relationship and defines the detailed practicality of the work to be done. It is distinguishable from the formal written contract of employment which, for the most part, only identifies mutual duties and responsibilities in a generalized form.

    a. Career
    b. Skilled worker
    c. Psychological contract
    d. Spatial mismatch

3. _____ has been described as the 'process of social influence in which one person can enlist the aid and support of others in the accomplishment of a common task' . A definition more inclusive of followers comes from Alan Keith of Genentech who said '_____ is ultimately about creating a way for people to contribute to making something extraordinary happen.'

_____ is one of the most salient aspects of the organizational context. However, defining _____ has been challenging.

    a. Situational leadership
    b. 1990 Clean Air Act
    c. Leadership
    d. 28-hour day

4. _____ is a civil designation for persons who are incorporated in a fixed or permanent way to a society or group: regular member of the working staff, permanent staff distinguished from a supernumerary.

The term '_____' and its counterpart, 'supernumerary,' originated in Spanish and Latin American academy and government; it is now also used in countries all over the world, such as France, the U.S., England, Italy, etc.

There are _____ members of surgical organizations, of universities, of gastronomical associations, etc.

a. Numerary
b. Adam Smith
c. Affiliation
d. Abraham Harold Maslow

1. '_____' refers to mental and communicative algorithms applied during social communications and interactions in order to reach certain effects or results. The term '_____' is used often in business contexts to refer to the measure of a person's ability to operate within business organizations through social communication and interactions. _____ are how people relate to one another.
   a. A4e
   b. AAAI
   c. A Stake in the Outcome
   d. Interpersonal skills

2. _____ is a subfield of the larger discipline of communication studies. _____, as a field, is the consideration, analysis, and criticism of the role of communication in organizational contexts.

   The field traces its lineage through business information, business communication, and early mass communication studies published in the 1930s through the 1950s.

   a. A4e
   b. A Stake in the Outcome
   c. AAAI
   d. Organizational communication

3. The _____ captures an expanded spectrum of values and criteria for measuring organizational success: economic, ecological and social. With the ratification of the United Nations and ICLEI _____ standard for urban and community accounting in early 2007, this became the dominant approach to public sector full cost accounting. Similar UN standards apply to natural capital and human capital measurement to assist in measurements required by _____, e.g. the ecoBudget standard for reporting ecological footprint.
   a. 33 Strategies of War
   b. Triple bottom line
   c. 28-hour day
   d. 1990 Clean Air Act

4. _____ describes the situation when output from (or information about the result of) an event or phenomenon in the past will influence the same event/phenomenon in the present or future. When an event is part of a chain of cause-and-effect that forms a circuit or loop, then the event is said to 'feed back' into itself.

   _____ is also a synonym for:

   - _____ signal; the information about the initial event that is the basis for subsequent modification of the event.
   - _____ loop; the causal path that leads from the initial generation of the _____ signal to the subsequent modification of the event.

_____ is a mechanism, process or signal that is looped back to control a system within itself. Such a loop is called a _____ loop.

a. 1990 Clean Air Act
b. Feedback loop
c. Positive feedback
d. Feedback

5. The 'business case for _____', theorizes that in a global marketplace, a company that employs a diverse workforce (both men and women, people of many generations, people from ethnically and racially diverse backgrounds etc.) is better able to understand the demographics of the marketplace it serves and is thus better equipped to thrive in that marketplace than a company that has a more limited range of employee demographics.

An additional corollary suggests that a company that supports the _____ of its workforce can also improve employee satisfaction, productivity and retention.

a. Kanban
b. Diversity
c. Virtual team
d. Trademark

6. _____ is a field of study that looks at how people from differing cultural backgrounds endeavour to communicate.

In years during and preceding the Cold War, the United States economy was largely self-contained because the world was polarized into two separate and competing powers: the east and west. However, changes and advancements in economic relationships, political systems, and technological options began to break down old cultural barriers.

a. 1990 Clean Air Act
b. Cross-cultural Communication
c. 33 Strategies of War
d. 28-hour day

7. The _____ is the labour pool in employment. It is generally used to describe those working for a single company or industry, but can also apply to a geographic region like a city, country, state, etc. The term generally excludes the employers or management, and implies those involved in manual labour.

a. Workforce
b. Pink-collar worker
c. Division of labour
d. Work-life balance

8. _____ refers to the long-term management of intractable conflicts. It is the label for the variety of ways by which people handle grievances--standing up for what they consider to be right and against what they consider to be wrong. Those ways include such diverse phenomena as gossip, ridicule, lynching, terrorism, warfare, feuding, genocide, law, mediation, and avoidance.
a. 1990 Clean Air Act
b. 33 Strategies of War
c. Conflict management
d. 28-hour day

9. _____ is a recursive process where two or more people or organizations work together in an intersection of common goals -- for example, an intellectual endeavor that is creative in nature--by sharing knowledge, learning and building consensus. _____ does not require leadership and can sometimes bring better results through decentralization and egalitarianism. In particular, teams that work collaboratively can obtain greater resources, recognition and reward when facing competition for finite resources._____ is also present in opposing goals exhibiting the notion of adversarial _____, though this is not a common case for using the term.
a. 1990 Clean Air Act
b. Collectivism
c. 28-hour day
d. Collaboration

10. _____ is an idea in the field of Organizational studies and management which describes the psychology, attitudes, experiences, beliefs and Values (personal and cultural values) of an organization. It has been defined as 'the specific collection of values and norms that are shared by people and groups in an organization and that control the way they interact with each other and with stakeholders outside the organization.'

This definition continues to explain organizational values also known as 'beliefs and ideas about what kinds of goals members of an organization should pursue and ideas about the appropriate kinds or standards of behavior organizational members should use to achieve these goals. From organizational values develop organizational norms, guidelines or expectations that prescribe appropriate kinds of behavior by employees in particular situations and control the behavior of organizational members towards one another.'

_____ is not the same as corporate culture.

a. Organizational culture
b. Union shop
c. Organizational effectiveness
d. Organizational development

11. _____ is a civil designation for persons who are incorporated in a fixed or permanent way to a society or group: regular member of the working staff, permanent staff distinguished from a supernumerary.

The term '_____' and its counterpart, 'supernumerary,' originated in Spanish and Latin American academy and government; it is now also used in countries all over the world, such as France, the U.S., England, Italy, etc.

There are _____ members of surgical organizations, of universities, of gastronomical associations, etc.

a. Numerary
b. Affiliation
c. Adam Smith
d. Abraham Harold Maslow

12. In game theory and economic theory, _____ describes a situation in which a participant's gain or loss is exactly balanced by the losses or gains of the other participant(s.) If the total gains of the participants are added up, and the total losses are subtracted, they will sum to zero. _____ can be thought of more generally as constant sum where the benefits and losses to all players sum to the same value of money and pride and dignity.
a. 33 Strategies of War
b. 1990 Clean Air Act
c. 28-hour day
d. Zero-sum

13. In finance, the _____s between two currencies specifies how much one currency is worth in terms of the other. It is the value of a foreign nation's currency in terms of the home nation's currency. For example an _____ of 102 Japanese yen to the United States dollar means that JPY 102 is worth the same as USD 1.
a. AAAI
b. A4e
c. Exchange rate
d. A Stake in the Outcome

14. _____ is an advertisement in which a particular product specifically mentions a competitor by name for the express purpose of showing why the competitor is inferior to the product naming it.

This should not be confused with parody advertisements, where a fictional product is being advertised for the purpose of poking fun at the particular advertisement, nor should it be confused with the use of a coined brand name for the purpose of comparing the product without actually naming an actual competitor. ('Wikipedia tastes better and is less filling than the Encyclopedia Galactica.')

In the 1980s, during what has been referred to as the cola wars, soft-drink manufacturer Pepsi ran a series of advertisements where people, caught on hidden camera, in a blind taste test, chose Pepsi over rival Coca-Cola.

  a. 33 Strategies of War
  b. 28-hour day
  c. Comparative advertising
  d. 1990 Clean Air Act

15. An arbitral tribunal (or arbitration tribunal) is a panel of one or more adjudicators which is convened and sits to resolve a dispute by way of arbitration. The tribunal may consist of a sole _____, or there may be two or more _____s, which might include either a chairman or an umpire. The parties to a dispute are usually free to agree the number and composition of the arbitral tribunal.
  a. AAAI
  b. A4e
  c. A Stake in the Outcome
  d. Arbitrator

16. _____ is one of the managerial functions like planning, organizing, staffing and directing. It is an important function because it helps to check the errors and to take the corrective action so that deviation from standards are minimized and stated goals of the organization are achieved in desired manner. According to modern concepts, _____ is a foreseeing action whereas earlier concept of _____ was used only when errors were detected. _____ in management means setting standards, measuring actual performance and taking corrective action.
  a. Decision tree pruning
  b. Schedule of reinforcement
  c. Turnover
  d. Control

17. _____ is one of the four elements of marketing mix. An organization or set of organizations (go-betweens) involved in the process of making a product or service available for use or consumption by a consumer or business user.

The other three parts of the marketing mix are product, pricing, and promotion.

a. Matching theory
b. Missing completely at random
c. Job creation programs
d. Distribution

18. In sociology and social psychology, _____ is the process through which people try to control the impressions other people form of them. It is a goal-directed conscious or unconscious attempt to influence the perceptions of other people about a person, object or event by regulating and controlling information in social interaction. It is usually used synonymously with self-presentation, if a person tries to influence the perception of their image.

a. Impression management
b. AAAI
c. A Stake in the Outcome
d. A4e

19. _____ refers to the movement of cash into or out of a business or financial product. It is usually measured during a specified, finite period of time. Measurement of _____ can be used

- to determine a project's rate of return or value. The time of _____s into and out of projects are used as inputs in financial models such as internal rate of return, and net present value.
- to determine problems with a business's liquidity. Being profitable does not necessarily mean being liquid. A company can fail because of a shortage of cash, even while profitable.
- as an alternate measure of a business's profits when it is believed that accrual accounting concepts do not represent economic realities. For example, a company may be notionally profitable but generating little operational cash (as may be the case for a company that barters its products rather than selling for cash.) In such a case, the company may be deriving additional operating cash by issuing shares evaluating default risk, re-investment requirements, etc.

_____ is a generic term used differently depending on the context. It may be defined by users for their own purposes.

a. Gross profit
b. Gross profit margin
c. Sweat equity
d. Cash flow

20. _____ is an integrated communications-based process through which individuals and communities discover that existing and newly-identified needs and wants may be satisfied by the products and services of others.

_____ is defined by the American _____ Association as the activity, set of institutions, and processes for creating, communicating, delivering, and exchanging offerings that have value for customers, clients, partners, and society at large. The term developed from the original meaning which referred literally to going to market, as in shopping, or going to a market to buy or sell goods or services.

a. Customer relationship management
b. Market development
c. Marketing
d. Disruptive technology

Chapter 18. Managing Change: Revisiting the Changing World of Work

1. _____ is a structured approach to transitioning individuals, teams, and organizations from a current state to a desired future state. The current definition of _____ includes both organizational _____ processes and individual _____ models, which together are used to manage the people side of change.

A number of models are available for understanding the transitioning of individuals through the phases of _____ and strengthening organizational development initiative in both government and corporate sectors.

   a. 28-hour day
   b. 33 Strategies of War
   c. 1990 Clean Air Act
   d. Change management

2. The _____ captures an expanded spectrum of values and criteria for measuring organizational success: economic, ecological and social. With the ratification of the United Nations and ICLEI _____ standard for urban and community accounting in early 2007, this became the dominant approach to public sector full cost accounting. Similar UN standards apply to natural capital and human capital measurement to assist in measurements required by _____, e.g. the ecoBudget standard for reporting ecological footprint.
   a. 33 Strategies of War
   b. 28-hour day
   c. Triple bottom line
   d. 1990 Clean Air Act

3. _____ is a civil designation for persons who are incorporated in a fixed or permanent way to a society or group: regular member of the working staff, permanent staff distinguished from a supernumerary.

The term '_____' and its counterpart, 'supernumerary,' originated in Spanish and Latin American academy and government; it is now also used in countries all over the world, such as France, the U.S., England, Italy, etc.

There are _____ members of surgical organizations, of universities, of gastronomical associations, etc.

   a. Numerary
   b. Adam Smith
   c. Abraham Harold Maslow
   d. Affiliation

4. In finance, the _____s between two currencies specifies how much one currency is worth in terms of the other. It is the value of a foreign nation's currency in terms of the home nation's currency. For example an _____ of 102 Japanese yen to the United States dollar means that JPY 102 is worth the same as USD 1.

a. A4e
b. AAAI
c. A Stake in the Outcome
d. Exchange rate

5. _____ is an advertisement in which a particular product specifically mentions a competitor by name for the express purpose of showing why the competitor is inferior to the product naming it.

This should not be confused with parody advertisements, where a fictional product is being advertised for the purpose of poking fun at the particular advertisement, nor should it be confused with the use of a coined brand name for the purpose of comparing the product without actually naming an actual competitor. ('Wikipedia tastes better and is less filling than the Encyclopedia Galactica.')

In the 1980s, during what has been referred to as the cola wars, soft-drink manufacturer Pepsi ran a series of advertisements where people, caught on hidden camera, in a blind taste test, chose Pepsi over rival Coca-Cola.

a. Comparative advertising
b. 1990 Clean Air Act
c. 33 Strategies of War
d. 28-hour day

6. _____ is an idea in the field of Organizational studies and management which describes the psychology, attitudes, experiences, beliefs and Values (personal and cultural values) of an organization. It has been defined as 'the specific collection of values and norms that are shared by people and groups in an organization and that control the way they interact with each other and with stakeholders outside the organization.'

This definition continues to explain organizational values also known as 'beliefs and ideas about what kinds of goals members of an organization should pursue and ideas about the appropriate kinds or standards of behavior organizational members should use to achieve these goals. From organizational values develop organizational norms, guidelines or expectations that prescribe appropriate kinds of behavior by employees in particular situations and control the behavior of organizational members towards one another.'

_____ is not the same as corporate culture.

a. Organizational effectiveness
b. Organizational development
c. Union shop
d. Organizational culture

Chapter 18. Managing Change: Revisiting the Changing World of Work   123

7. _____ describes the situation when output from (or information about the result of) an event or phenomenon in the past will influence the same event/phenomenon in the present or future. When an event is part of a chain of cause-and-effect that forms a circuit or loop, then the event is said to 'feed back' into itself.

_____ is also a synonym for:

- _____ signal; the information about the initial event that is the basis for subsequent modification of the event.
- _____ loop; the causal path that leads from the initial generation of the _____ signal to the subsequent modification of the event.

_____ is a mechanism, process or signal that is looped back to control a system within itself. Such a loop is called a _____ loop.

   a. Feedback loop
   b. Positive feedback
   c. 1990 Clean Air Act
   d. Feedback

8. As defined by Richard Beckhard, _____ is a planned, top-down, organization-wide effort to increase the organization's effectiveness and health. _____ is achieved through interventions in the organization's 'processes,' using behavioural science knowledge. According to Warren Bennis, _____ is a complex strategy intended to change the beliefs, attitudes, values, and structure of organizations so that they can better adapt to new technologies, markets, and challenges.
   a. Informal organization
   b. Organizational structure
   c. Organizational culture
   d. Organizational development

9. The _____ is the labour pool in employment. It is generally used to describe those working for a single company or industry, but can also apply to a geographic region like a city, country, state, etc. The term generally excludes the employers or management, and implies those involved in manual labour.
   a. Pink-collar worker
   b. Work-life balance
   c. Division of labour
   d. Workforce

10. _____ is one of the managerial functions like planning, organizing, staffing and directing. It is an important function because it helps to check the errors and to take the corrective action so that deviation from standards are minimized and stated goals of the organization are achieved in desired manner.According to modern concepts, _____ is a foreseeing action whereas earlier concept of _____ was used only when errors were detected. _____ in management means setting standards, measuring actual performance and taking corrective action.
   a. Schedule of reinforcement
   b. Control
   c. Turnover
   d. Decision tree pruning

11. _____ can be regarded as an outcome of mental processes (cognitive process) leading to the selection of a course of action among several alternatives. Every _____ process produces a final choice. The output can be an action or an opinion of choice.
   a. 1990 Clean Air Act
   b. 33 Strategies of War
   c. 28-hour day
   d. Decision making

12. _____ is the temporary suspension or permanent termination of employment of an employee or (more commonly) a group of employees for business reasons, such as the decision that certain positions are no longer necessary or a business slow-down or interruption in work. Originally the term '_____' referred exclusively to a temporary interruption in work, as when factory work cyclically falls off. However, in recent times the term can also refer to the permanent elimination of a position.
   a. Retirement
   b. Wrongful dismissal
   c. Layoff
   d. Termination of employment

13. _____ is a subfield of the larger discipline of communication studies. _____, as a field, is the consideration, analysis, and criticism of the role of communication in organizational contexts.

The field traces its lineage through business information, business communication, and early mass communication studies published in the 1930s through the 1950s.

   a. A4e
   b. Organizational Communication
   c. AAAI
   d. A Stake in the Outcome

Chapter 18. Managing Change: Revisiting the Changing World of Work

14. A _____ is the term given to a company that facilitates the learning of its members and continuously transforms itself. _____s develop as a result of the pressures facing modern organizations and enables them to remain competitive in the business environment. A _____ has five main features; systems thinking, personal mastery, mental models, shared vision and team learning.
    a. 1990 Clean Air Act
    b. Hoshin Kanri
    c. Learning organization
    d. Quality function deployment

15. In probability theory, a probability distribution is called _____ if its cumulative distribution function is _____. This is equivalent to saying that for random variables X with the distribution in question, Pr[X = a] = 0 for all real numbers a, i.e.: the probability that X attains the value a is zero, for any number a. If the distribution of X is _____ then X is called a _____ random variable.
    a. Decision tree pruning
    b. Connectionist expert systems
    c. Pay Band
    d. Continuous

16. A _____ is a subset of the overall internal controls of a business covering the application of people, documents, technologies, and procedures by management accountants to solving business problems such as costing a product, service or a business-wide strategy. _____s are distinct from regular information systems in that they are used to analyze other information systems applied in operational activities in the organization. Academically, the term is commonly used to refer to the group of information management methods tied to the automation or support of human decision making, e.g. Decision Support Systems, Expert systems, and Executive information systems.
    a. Strategic information system
    b. Management information system
    c. 28-hour day
    d. 1990 Clean Air Act

17. The _____ was a period in the late 18th and early 19th centuries when major changes in agriculture, manufacturing, mining, and transportation had a profound effect on the socioeconomic and cultural conditions in Britain. The changes subsequently spread throughout Europe, North America, and eventually the world. The onset of the _____ marked a major turning point in human society; almost every aspect of daily life was eventually influenced in some way.
    a. Adam Smith
    b. Affiliation
    c. Abraham Harold Maslow
    d. Industrial revolution

Chapter 18. Managing Change: Revisiting the Changing World of Work

18. In a military context, the _____ is the line of authority and responsibility along which orders are passed within a military unit and between different units. The term is also used in a civilian management context describing comparable hierarchical structures of authority.
   a. 1990 Clean Air Act
   b. French leave
   c. Chain of command
   d. 28-hour day

19. _____ Movement refers to those researchers of organizational development who study the behavior of people in groups, in particular workplace groups. It originated in the 1920s' Hawthorne studies, which examined the effects of social relations, motivation and employee satisfaction on factory productivity. The movement viewed workers in terms of their psychology and fit with companies, rather than as interchangeable parts.
   a. Participatory management
   b. Human relations
   c. Work design
   d. Hersey-Blanchard situational theory

20. _____ refers to those researchers of organizational development who study the behavior of people in groups, in particular workplace groups. It originated in the 1920s' Hawthorne studies, which examined the effects of social relations, motivation and employee satisfaction on factory productivity. The movement viewed workers in terms of their psychology and fit with companies, rather than as interchangeable parts.
   a. Job satisfaction
   b. Path-goal theory
   c. Job analysis
   d. Human relations movement

21. _____ consists of the mental process of thinking involved with the process of judging the merits of multiple options and selecting one of them for action. Some simple examples include deciding whether to get up in the morning or go back to sleep, or selecting a given route for a journey. More complex examples (often decisions that affect what a person thinks or their core beliefs) include choosing a lifestyle, religious affiliation, or political position.
   a. Trade study
   b. Championship mobilization
   c. Groups decision making
   d. Choice

22. _____ is used to assign the available resources in an economic way. It is part of resource management.

In strategic planning, is a plan for using available resources, for example human resources, especially in the near term, to achieve goals for the future.

a. 1990 Clean Air Act
b. 28-hour day
c. 33 Strategies of War
d. Resource allocation

Chapter 1
1. d	2. d	3. c	4. b	5. a	6. b	7. b	8. d	9. d	10. c
11. d	12. b	13. c	14. d	15. c	16. a	17. d	18. d	19. d	20. d
21. d	22. c	23. c	24. a	25. d	26. b	27. d			

Chapter 2
1. d	2. b	3. a	4. d	5. b	6. d	7. a	8. b	9. b	10. a
11. d	12. a	13. a	14. c	15. c	16. a	17. d	18. b	19. a	20. a
21. a	22. d								

Chapter 3
1. b	2. d	3. b	4. d	5. b	6. d	7. b	8. a	9. d	10. d
11. c	12. d	13. c	14. d	15. d	16. d	17. b	18. d	19. d	20. a
21. b	22. b	23. d							

Chapter 4
1. d	2. a	3. d	4. b	5. d	6. b	7. a	8. d	9. d	10. d
11. a	12. d	13. d	14. c	15. d	16. a	17. d	18. a	19. b	20. b
21. d									

Chapter 5
1. d	2. d	3. d	4. d	5. a	6. d	7. d	8. d	9. d	10. d
11. d	12. d	13. a	14. a	15. d	16. d	17. c	18. a	19. d	20. b
21. d									

Chapter 6
1. d	2. c	3. a	4. c	5. a	6. b	7. d	8. c	9. c	10. a
11. c	12. d	13. a	14. b	15. b	16. c	17. d	18. d	19. b	20. d
21. a	22. d	23. d	24. d	25. d	26. d				

Chapter 7
1. d	2. d	3. d	4. c	5. b	6. d	7. d	8. a	9. d	10. b
11. a	12. d	13. b	14. c	15. d	16. a	17. a	18. a	19. b	20. d
21. c	22. d	23. b	24. c	25. d	26. d	27. d	28. a	29. b	30. c
31. d	32. d	33. a	34. d						

Chapter 8
1. d	2. d	3. c	4. d	5. a	6. d	7. d	8. c	9. d	10. d
11. d	12. d	13. d	14. d	15. b	16. c	17. d	18. c		

Chapter 9
1. d	2. a	3. d	4. d	5. c	6. a	7. d	8. b	9. b	10. a
11. c	12. c	13. a	14. a	15. d	16. b	17. c	18. a	19. c	20. d
21. d	22. d	23. d	24. d	25. d	26. d	27. a	28. a	29. c	30. d
31. a	32. d	33. b	34. d	35. d	36. d	37. c	38. d	39. c	40. c
41. d	42. c	43. d	44. d	45. a	46. b	47. a	48. b	49. c	

ANSWER KEY

Chapter 10
1. c   2. a   3. d   4. b   5. b   6. a   7. b   8. b   9. d   10. b
11. c   12. d   13. d   14. d   15. b   16. d   17. a   18. d

Chapter 11
1. d   2. b   3. d   4. b   5. c   6. a

Chapter 12
1. a   2. a   3. d   4. a   5. d   6. d   7. c   8. a   9. c   10. d
11. a   12. a   13. d   14. c   15. d   16. d   17. d   18. b   19. d   20. b
21. d   22. a   23. d   24. c   25. a   26. d

Chapter 13
1. b   2. a   3. d   4. d   5. c   6. d   7. d   8. a   9. a   10. b
11. a   12. d   13. a   14. a   15. a   16. c   17. d   18. b   19. d   20. d
21. b   22. c   23. b   24. d   25. d

Chapter 14
1. d   2. a   3. d   4. d   5. d   6. d   7. d   8. c   9. c   10. d

Chapter 15
1. b   2. d   3. b   4. d   5. d   6. d   7. d   8. d   9. c

Chapter 16
1. c   2. c   3. c   4. a

Chapter 17
1. d   2. d   3. b   4. d   5. b   6. b   7. a   8. c   9. d   10. a
11. a   12. d   13. c   14. c   15. d   16. d   17. d   18. a   19. d   20. c

Chapter 18
1. d   2. c   3. a   4. d   5. a   6. d   7. d   8. d   9. d   10. b
11. d   12. c   13. b   14. c   15. d   16. b   17. d   18. c   19. b   20. d
21. d   22. d